PATRICIA TANUMIHARDJA

FARM to TABLE
ASIAN SECRETS

VEGAN & VEGETARIAN FULL-FLAVORED RECIPES FOR EVERY SEASON

TUTTLE Publishing

Tokyo | Rutland, Vermont | Singapore

Contents

Autumn Recipes

Winter Recipes

(**V** = Vegan; **GF** = Gluten Free; **V*** and **GF*** denote recipes that can be made egg, honey and gluten free, respectively; with substitutions)

Preparing Seasonal Vegetables the Flavorful Asian Way

When I was growing up in Singapore, I didn't yet understand the concept of eating and cooking seasonally, or what is now known in the U.S. as the "farm-to-table" movement. The tropical climate meant we only had two "seasons"—hot and wet, and hot and dry. And since the island-state imported most of its food, many of the same items were available year-round (except for the "King of Fruits," the durian, which I looked forward to every June and December). My childhood meals usually consisted of white rice accompanied by one or two vegetable dishes, an egg, meat or fish dish, and/or a soup. One-pot meals like *nasi goreng* (Indonesian fried rice) and *mee soto* (noodles in turmeric-spiced broth) featured rice or noodles studded with tiny bits of meat and showered with fresh vegetables, herbs, spices and chilies. This diet is a perfect example of the peripheral role meat plays in the average Asian diet.

When I moved to Seattle for college, I was shocked to learn that many of the fresh fruits and vegetables I had taken for granted back home were hard to come by. And even when available, they were only sold at certain times

of year. In their place I found strange items like fennel, crookneck squash and parsnips. My introduction to the seasonal food-growing cycle was also a rude awakening, but I quickly learned to adapt.

Today, my edible inclinations stem both from my cultural upbringing and a conscious lifestyle choice. My affinity for seasonal produce grown by local farmers developed while managing a farmer's market in Pacific Grove, California. I was at the market every week, getting to know the people who grew my food and discovering all their wonderful locally grown produce. Friendly farmers gave me samples of their best wares, and cooking suggestions were always forthcoming. I was taught to sauté Swiss chard with potatoes and onions and wrap this filling up in fresh tortillas. I learned to peel and slice broccoli stems and toss them with a red-wine vinaigrette dressing to make a crunchy and delicious salad. As a result, I'm a full-fledged, card-carrying member of the farm-to-table club, eating whatever is grown locally according to the rhythm of the seasons.

I bring my son to the farmer's market to show him how to select fresh produce.

Red and Golden Beets in Green Curry (page 106)

My mom, Juliana, taught me the finer points of Indonesian cooking. I still defer to her.

The benefits of local and seasonal eating are manifold, including grocery savings and a smaller carbon footprint. Foods in season are harvested and sold at the peak of their availability, making them cheaper to harvest and transport. But most of all, foods in season are at their freshest and most flavorful. Japanese food expert Hiroko Shimbo uses the term *shun* to describe the magic moment when ingredients are at peak quality. For example, asparagus becomes shun in early summer when they are bursting with flavor, and tender and juicy. Spicy-crisp daikon radish is shun in winter, as are sugar-sweet English peas in springtime.

The Asian Spark

I've always known that Asian cultures approach vegetables with creativity and spark. This is no coincidence, as much of Asian cooking is authentically vegetarian— and very often vegan.

The key to cooking vegetables is understanding how to blend flavors, textures, aromas and colors— all trademarks of Asian cooking— to create dishes that truly sing.

Asian cooks tend to combine contrary flavors, and love to play with the four basic tastes of sweet, sour, salty and bitter. If you've had a bowl of tom yum soup or a plate of sweet-and-sour pork, you'll agree that Asian cooks are masters at balancing these tastes to create a culinary symphony.

The fifth taste, umami, is another important component in Asian cooking. The word umami has been used in Japan for hundreds of years to signify something delicious. Yet umami's true qualities remain elusive. Simply put, umami is the satisfying flavor of protein— which makes everything delicious.

"Secrets" of Asian Cooking

Think of this cookbook as an Asian cooking "tell-all" sharing secrets used throughout Asia to make dishes more flavorful and more nuanced.

Here's a sneak peek:

Harmonizing the contrasting flavors of ingredients like palm sugar (sweet), soy sauce (salty), tamarind juice (sour), and chili paste (spicy) elevates a vegetable dish from ordinary to oh-so delicious.

My mom invented a *yu sheng* (raw fish salad) for our Lunar New Year celebration.

Vegetables and Egg Donburi Rice Bowl (page 112)

Fun on Portland, OR, KATU's "AM Northwest," cooking with the late Dave Anderson.

Umami enhances the flavor of vegetables without overpowering their delicate natural flavor. Meat and dairy products are naturally umami-packed. Vegan options include umami-laden ingredients like sea vegetables and produce such as tomatoes and mushrooms. And let's not forget fermented products like soy sauce, kimchi and fermented beans or miso.

Infused oils are another easy way to boost the flavor of vegetable dishes. Oils infused with garlic, onion and chili are commonly used in Asian cooking—just a few drizzles can add a whole new flavor dimension to any dish.

Furthermore, Asian cooks have always known that texture is a turn-on. Fried shallots, crispy garlic slices, and crunchy pickles not only inject lots of flavor, but also impart a contrasting texture in the mouth that makes a dish more appetizing and interesting to eat.

Think of fried spring rolls; when you bite into a roll, the crisp shell shatters to reveal the moist, shredded vegetable filling. And doesn't a forkful from a Vietnamese noodle bowl—crunchy pickles, firm fried tofu, slippery noodles and soft mushrooms—feel like a party in your mouth?

Local Vegetables, Asian Flavors

Many Asian vegetarian cookbooks that have come before simply replace the meat in a recipe with tofu. However, this cookbook shines the spotlight on vegetables. I also wanted to answer the question, "How do you prepare local vegetables the Asian way to maximize their flavors?"

Vegetables like bok choy, Chinese (napa) cabbage and pea shoots are a common sight in farmer's markets and supermarkets; others, like bitter melon and Chinese flowering cabbage (*choy sum*) are harder to find. On the other hand, tables at farmers' markets are buckling under the weight of locally grown vegetables such as beets, butternut squash and purple potatoes. Although not common in traditional Asian cooking, these vegetables are equally versatile and delicious, and can be prepared in similar ways to Asian vegetables. You just need to learn to mix and match cooking techniques and flavors with each vegetable.

Fortunately, you don't need special equipment to cook the Asian way, and basic Asian sauces, herbs and spices are now sold everywhere. Most cities also have a health-food store or Asian

Peppery Turmeric Soup (page 126)

market where an even wider range of Asian ingredients is available.

Adapting traditional recipes to locally available ingredients is nothing new for immigrants, least of all my mom. I've often seen her work her magic in the kitchen, substituting kale for yam leaves, or experimenting with zucchini.

Taking my mom's lead, I use Asian methods of preparation like steaming and stir-frying, and quintessential herbs and seasonings like ginger and palm sugar. But my cooking style is informed by Western sensibilities.

I'll demonstrate how easy it is to combine the very freshest produce with the Asian flavors you love—in recipes such as Egg Flower Soup with English Peas and Sweet Corn, Red Curry Noodles with Roasted Cauliflower and Rainbow Carrots, and General Tso's Eggplant.

You'll have ample "tools" to stash in your cooking arsenal; you can wield them whether you're cooking Chinese broccoli or broccoli raab.

With practice, you'll soon recognize how to apply various cooking techniques and preparations to specific seasonal vegetables.

I hope my original ideas and creative flavor combinations will help you "think outside the wok," and encourage you to dig into your weekly CSA (Community Supported Agriculture) box and/or buy from a local farmer.

Pan-Asian Recipes

The recipes in this cookbook span East and Southeast Asia—familiar territory for me because of my background. I am of Chinese descent, but I was born in Indonesia and raised in Singapore. Thus, I am accustomed to eating a wide variety of different Southeast Asian foods, and over the years have traveled, researched and eaten my way throughout Asia. I have come to appreciate the cuisines of Japan, Vietnam, Indonesia, Malaysia, India, Thailand and the Philippines, among others. Plus, my research for my previous book, *The*

Stir-Fried Cellophane Noodles (page 110)

Asian Grandmothers' Cookbook, gave me an opportunity to learn firsthand from women who are experts in these cuisines.

Regardless of where the recipes originate, almost all of the ingredients in this book can be easily purchased. When I believe a certain exotic flavor is essential to a dish, I offer close substitutes. These dishes may not be truly "authentic," but they're just as tasty as the dishes that inspired them!

The Goals of This Book

Even though I have professional culinary training, I'm a home cook at heart. To reflect this philosophy, I have created straightforward, flavorful dishes—the kind I make for my own family regularly. My recipes are designed for regular folks who don't want to spend too much time in the kitchen but still want to eat well.

As you'll discover in this book, home-cooked Asian food is very different from what you find at most Asian restaurants in the U.S. With just a few staple ingredients and simple tricks of the trade, you, too, can cook delicious Asian-style vegetable dishes.

Many recipes can be completed in 30 to 45 minutes; a few require slightly more time and energy. In these cases, I have indicated the steps that can be done ahead. All in all, you'll find plenty of recipes suitable for weekday meals, as well as options for a leisurely weekend of cooking with friends or entertaining without lots of fuss.

Overall, I had three goals in mind as I wrote:

1. To show vegetarians, vegans and omnivores (and perhaps even ardent carnivores) that vegetable-focused meals can be incredibly tasty and satisfying.

2. To encourage you to learn a few "secret" Asian techniques and tricks, and not just follow recipes blindly. This way, you can adjust your cooking to the availability of ingredients. Be creative—many ingredients have similar flavor profiles, so substitutions are your allies!

3. To demystify Asian cooking. It's easy—and quick—once you know a few basic techniques and understand the method behind the madness. You'll save money on takeout, and you'll impress your family and friends!

With that, I leave you to explore and experiment. I hope you'll enjoy learning how to create vegetable-focused meals with Asian flavors to suit your palate and to satisfy your appetite.

Flaky Chinese Pancakes with Chive Blossoms (page 48)

Patricia Tanumihardja

Seasonal Variations

I have a collection of favorite recipes that I like to make year round by simply substituting other vegetables that are at the peak of their flavor. Here are some of my seasonal variations on recipes in this book.

RECIPE	SPRING	SUMMER	AUTUMN	WINTER
Dumplings (page 100)	Leeks and cellophane noodles	Tomato, chives and egg	Fennel, carrots and egg	Cabbage, mushrooms and tofu
Fried Rice (page 63)	English peas Pea shoots	Zucchini Tomatoes	Kale Chanterelles	Rainbow chard Cauliflower
Red Curry (page 54)	Asparagus Fava beans	Red peppers Eggplant Tomatoes	Kabocha, delicata or acorn squash	Sweet potato Parsnips Kale
Greens with Sesame Sauce (page 54)	Fiddlehead ferns Dandelion greens	Spinach Chrysanthemum leaves	Swiss or rainbow chard	Red Russian kale
Spring Rolls (page 50)	Bamboo shoots and mushrooms	Zucchini and fennel	Celery root and carrots	Turnip and carrots

Seasonal Menu Suggestions

When planning your menus, it is important to think about how the flavors and textures will work with one another. For example, if you choose a spicy dish, contrast that with one that is more bland. Or if you chose a dish with lots of sauce, combine that with a drier dish. There are so many different types of rice available on the market today: red rice, pink rice, green-tea rice, black forbidden rice, and so on. Each of them has distinct qualities that make them suitable for different occasions and seasons. Here are some ideas for family-style menus.

SEASON	STARTER	RICE	MAIN DISH 1	MAIN DISH 2
SPRING	Crispy Spring Rolls (page 50)	Jasmine brown rice	Fresh Artichoke Hearts, Green Beans and Bell Pepper in Thai Red Curry (page 54)	Broccolini with Seasoned Soy Sauce (page 57)
SUMMER	Fresh Salad with Sweet, Sour, Spicy Sauce (page 70)	Pink rice	Spicy Fried Okra (page 83)	Grilled Vegetable Kebabs with Two Marinades (page 76)
AUTUMN	Green Apple Salad with Tangy Thai Dressing (page 94)	Sticky (glutinous) rice	Red and Golden Beets in Green Curry (page 106)	Cherry Tomatoes Simmered with Tofu (page 107)
WINTER	Tofu, Spinach and Fennel Wontons (page 118)	Red rice	Roasted Brussels Sprouts with Sweet Chili Sauce (page 128)	Sweet Soy and Black Pepper Cauliflower (page 129)

Equipment and Utensils

You don't need exotic equipment to cook Asian food—only a minimum of utensils, many of which are already found in a Western kitchen. If you do own a wok or a bamboo steamer, by all means use them. Here's what I use regularly:

2¼-quart Dutch oven

2-quart saucepan and cast iron skillet

14-inch wok with lid

2-quart saucepan and cast iron skillet

Wok

The wok is the most versatile cooking vessel in my kitchen. I use it mostly for stir-frying, but also for deep-frying, steaming and much, much more. Mine is a 14-inch (35-cm) carbon steel wok, which is perfect for home cooking for a family of four. A flat-bottomed wok works best for electric ranges; a round-bottomed one is best for gas. They're great, but there's no need to buy a wok if you don't have one already (although you could put it on your wish list). A large skillet or sauté pan also works fine for stir-frying.

Cast-Iron Frying Pans

I have two cast-iron frying pans: A small one (6½ in/16.5 cm) for toasting seeds and spices, and a larger one (10 in/25 cm) for frying sunny-side-up eggs, pancakes, potstickers and more.

Dutch Oven

My two Dutch ovens (2.2 quart/liter and 3.75 quart/liter) bring cheer to my kitchen with their bright red color. Aesthetics aside, they are very useful for braising, making curries, congee, soups and stews, and deep-frying too! I prefer using the smaller vessel for deep-frying, even though it holds fewer items at a time. It lets me better control how quickly the food (spring rolls, green beans, etc.) cooks, and I use less oil. A heavy-bottomed saucepan or pot can do the same job.

Pots

If pots could talk, my trusty 6-quart/liter stainless-steel stockpot would have lots of stories to tell, mainly about stocks—vegetable, mushroom, chicken...you name it. Yes, I make stock in it, and congee as well. It makes a great steamer, too, whether with my steamer basket (above right), which

fits inside perfectly, or by channeling MacGyver (see page 14).

I have smaller 2- to 3-quart/liter pots with tight-fitting lids, which I use for cooking rice on the stovetop and boiling noodles in single-serve quantities.

Steamer Basket

Ever since I burned a hole in the bottom of my mom's metal steamer (always, always check to make sure there's enough water in your steamer), I've relied on my steamer basket. Made from stainless steel, it expands from 6 to 9 inches (15 to 23 cm) and fits a wide variety of pots. At its widest, the basket holds six to eight dumplings at a time, which is fine by me. To make it non-stick, I'll brush it with oil or cut out a piece of parchment to size.

Wooden Spatulas

The wooden spatula is my favorite cooking utensil—I have about six of them in different sizes and shapes! You may have heard that a metal wok spatula is ideal for stir-frying, because it has a wide shovel shape that matches the curved surface of a wok. Personally, I find it heavy and cumbersome, not least because the handle keeps falling off!

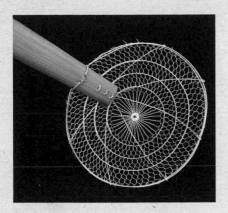

Wire-mesh Skimmer

My long-handled wire-mesh skimmer is another favorite tool. I use it for deep-frying, as well as for removing noodles, wontons, dumplings, etc. from boiling water. The wire mesh allows oil to drain from the food, and the long handle helps protect your hand from the heat. However, a slotted spoon can work just as well.

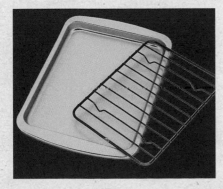

Wire Rack Sheet

After deep-frying things—sometimes even after pan-frying bacon or other greasy foods—I always drain them to get rid of excess oil. My go-to method was always paper towels until I bought a wire rack and set it atop a baking sheet. I discovered that the food turns out less soggy this way.

Food Processor

When I was a little girl, I would sit by my mom on the kitchen floor as she pounded herbs and spices into a smooth paste in her stone mortar. She would methodically add the firmer, more fibrous herbs like turmeric and lemongrass first, followed by hard spices like coriander and cumin, and finally the softer ingredients like garlic and shallots. It looked like a lot of work! Nowadays, she just uses a food processor, and I've followed suit. My 4-cup (1-liter) food processor is perfect for grinding spice pastes and making sauces. Any bigger, and your ingredients won't be ground properly. Use a spatula to scrape down the sides and add water a little at a time if the paste does not turn over as expected. Be observant and keep checking the consistency of the paste between your fingers.

Mortar and Pestle

When my parents first moved to the U.S. in 2002, my mom packed her 8-inch (20-cm) stone mortar and pestle in her suitcase. It just goes to show how important this tool was to her. However, since she no longer has the energy to spend 30 minutes pounding spice pastes, she gifted it to me. I use it to make *sambal oelek* and other simple fresh chili-based pastes. Most of the time, it sits on my shelf looking pretty.

I also have a small, lightweight Japanese ceramic mortar called a *suribachi*, which is paired with a wooden pestle called a *surikogi*. Mine is 5 inches (12.5 cm) in diameter and has a nubby lid that doubles as a ginger/garlic grater; the ridged interior is efficient for grinding small quantities of seeds and spices, and for crushing nuts.

Matchstick Peeler

I'm not usually one for single-job kitchen tools, but I couldn't do without my matchstick peeler for cutting thin strips of vegetables and fruits. I use it for zucchini, carrots, cucumber, apples and so much more. Shredding or cutting vegetables into matchsticks by hand isn't hard, though; it just takes a little longer.

Ginger Grater

I love my ginger grater! I no longer have to peel and mince fresh ginger into itty-bitty pieces with a knife. Plus, I don't even have to peel the ginger first, as most of the peel and fiber comes away during grating. You may already have a microplane grater in your kitchen, and that will work just as well.

Cooking Tips and Techniques

You don't have to go to culinary school to learn Asian cooking techniques. They are easy to learn; with practice, you'll be proficient in no time. All you need are a few simple implements and tools you likely already have in your kitchen.

Steaming

Fill the steaming vessel (the bottom part) with a generous amount of water, perhaps 3 to 4 inches (7.5 to 10 cm) or as much water as it can comfortably accommodate. You don't want the water to touch the bottom of the steamer basket or plate.

Monitor the water level and replenish with boiling water if it gets precariously low before the food is cooked.

Place a kitchen towel under the lid to absorb condensation. This will prevent the water from dripping onto your food and making it soggy.

When the food is done, turn off the heat and wait for the steam to subside before lifting the lid. Lift it away from you so you don't scald yourself, and so that condensation doesn't drip onto the food.

You don't have to buy a steamer to steam foods properly. You can easily steam most foods in a stockpot with a pasta insert or an asparagus steamer. Or experiment with common kitchen implements you already have. All you need is a vessel to hold water, a way to suspend the food over the water, and a lid to keep the steam in (visit my blog: picklesandtea.org for more information). Here are two ideas:

Crisscross two wooden chopsticks inside a wok or pot and add enough water to reach just below the chopsticks. Bring to a boil and balance a shallow dish or pie plate on the chopsticks.

Place a trivet or a small upturned bowl in a wok or a big, wide pot. Place a shallow dish or pie plate on top. Add enough water to reach just below the trivet—don't submerge it. And don't worry if you hear the bowl or trivet knocking against the bottom of the wok as the water boils.

Deep-Frying

The oil should be 1½ to 2 inches (4 to 5 cm) deep in your pan (between 2 and 3 cups/500 to 750 ml of oil for a 14-inch/35-cm wok) so that the food can be fully immersed in the oil and float freely as it cooks.

Select an oil with a high smoke point—sunflower and peanut oil are good choices.

Buy a deep-fry thermometer to track optimum temperature; a candy thermometer works, too. For a visual indicator, dip a wooden chopstick into the oil; if bubbles gather around it, the oil should be hot enough. You can also test-fry a bread cube or a small portion of what you're cooking—it should bubble gracefully to the surface and sizzle gently. If it just sits there soaking up oil, wait a couple more minutes before starting.

Fry in batches so as to not overcrowd the pan. Overcrowding lowers the oil temperature and may lead to splattering or spillage.

Battered foods often leave debris in the oil. Use a slotted spoon or a wire-mesh strainer to remove leftover fried bits, and then bring the oil temperature back up again before frying next batch.

Stir-Frying

Always preheat your wok or pan to achieve good wok-searing action and to dry up any water droplets. I generally heat my wok to medium-high heat and then raise or lower it if I need to.

How do you know it's ready? Sprinkle some water onto the wok. The beads should dance on the surface and vaporize within a couple of seconds. You'll

Chopsticks have many uses—I can even use them to lift a collapsible steamer basket.

also see a wisp or two of smoke.

After adding oil, throw in your first ingredient, usually garlic. If it sizzles gently and bubbles gather around its edges, you're ready to go. If it fries aggressively and starts burning, the oil is too hot. If it sits still, the oil isn't hot enough.

If the oil gets too hot and starts to smoke uncontrollably, remove the pan from the heat for a few seconds and lower the heat.

Don't overcrowd the pan. Putting too many ingredients in the pan lowers the temperature, and the foods will steam instead of sear. Add ingredients gradually, in small handfuls.

Adjust the heat after adding colder foods or liquids. Listen to the sizzle in your pan. If you hear too much sizzle, decrease the temperature; too little sizzle, increase the temperature.

Keep things moving swiftly around the wok; slide your spatula to the bottom and turn and toss ingredients up and over one another.

TO MARKET, TO MARKET!

Many people, me included, shop for ingredients fully intending to cook them. But life often gets in the way, and produce goes bad. Unfortunately, fresh vegetables and herbs don't freeze well, so you have to use them up before they go bad. I got tired of wasting food, so I came up with some strategies for buying and storing produce efficiently.

Planning Your Meals

Make a list of the recipes you want to try. Then pick out recipes that have common ingredients and group them accordingly. Many of the recipes in this cookbook use aromatics like garlic, ginger, onions and shallots. Note them down and you'll be able to prep everything at the same time.

Shopping

Create a shopping list based on your recipes, doubling or tripling ingredients as needed. Before you head out, determine what you have and what you need to buy, and clear out your fridge to make room for perishables.

At the store, pick up nonperishable items before you head to the produce aisle, especially if you're buying fragile produce. Get home as soon as possible and refrigerate your fruits and vegetables. If you'll be running errands between the market and your kitchen, keep a cooler in the car.

Shop farmers' markets early. Just-harvested greens wilt rapidly after a few hours in the sun.

Prepping

Cutting vegetables ahead of time isn't ideal. But if you're a busy working parent, or work late nights, having ready-chopped ingredients in the fridge means you'll be more likely to cook dinner at home than buy takeout. This advance prep also means dinner will be on the table faster. If it suits you, set aside part of your weekend for vegetable prep to save time during the week. Divide cut ingredients up according to each recipe. Then bag, pack, label and refrigerate in glass containers or zip-top bags as you go.

Storing

Leave refrigerated produce unwashed in its original packaging or wrapped loosely in a plastic bag. (Exceptions: place leafy herbs in a glass of water and cover with a plastic bag, and store mushrooms in a brown paper bag).

If storing fruits and vegetables at room temperature, remove from packaging and leave loose.

Eat Perishable Produce First

Here are some examples:

Eat first: asparagus, corn, green beans, mushrooms

Second: arugula, eggplant, cucumbers, zucchini

Third: bell peppers, cauliflower, leeks, spinach, tomatoes

Last: cabbage, carrots, potatoes, winter squash

Farmers' markets offer a bounty of locally produced fruits and veggies.

My son enjoys helping me in the kitchen with meal prep.

MY ASIAN PANTRY

These are tried-and-true Asian ingredients that I always have on hand. Fortunately, many sauces and pastes are pretty similar across cultures, so I just buy one type instead of having, say, both Japanese *shoyu* and Chinese soy sauce. I try to buy these essentials at an Asian market because they're usually cheaper there, but some variation of all the items listed should be available in the Asian/International aisle at your local supermarket. If not, you can also find them at a specialty market like Whole Foods or Trader Joe's (or online). This section describes only a fraction of all the ingredients used in Asian cooking. It would take whole volume to cover them all, so only the ingredients used in this book are included here.

CHINESE BLACK VINEGAR Also called Chinkiang black vinegar, this can be made from rice or other grains such as wheat, millet or sorghum. The best ones have a complex, smoky flavor developed over years of aging, reminiscent of a good Italian balsamic vinegar, which is a great substitute. My favorite brand, Gold Plum, is found in the bottled sauce aisle of the Asian market.

CHINESE COOKING WINE This aromatic cooking wine, also known as Shaoxing rice wine, is made by fermenting glutinous rice. I add it in moderation to marinades, braises and stir-fries for a little kick. I like LinChen's Michiu brand from California, but any additive-free brand will do. If I can't make it to the Asian store, I'll buy a bottle of pale dry sherry as a substi-

Chilies

Chilies are a very important component of Asian cooking, adding both aroma and heat. Try to obtain a good balance of the two when selecting chilies, remembering that size and color are not good indicators of their potency. In all the recipes in this book, the amount of chilies you use is up to your discretion. The seeds are the most potent part of the chili, so remove them as desired. One caveat: Don't add so much chili that you cannot taste the sweet, salty and sour flavors that make up a dish.

DRIED RED CHILIES Dried chilies abound, but the small red ones used in Asian cooking tend to be arbol or Japanese chilies. Both are spicy, measuring no longer than 3 to 4 inches (7.5 to 10 cm). Use them whole, ground, crushed or roasted, with or without their seeds. Store them in an airtight container in a cool, dark place.

LONG RED CHILIES You'll find an assortment of long red chilies ranging in length from 4 to 8 inches (10 to 20 cm) at the Asian market. Most are nameless, and the only way to gauge their flavor is to try them. At the grocery store, you might find Fresno (sometimes called red jalapeno), cayenne, or Anaheim chilies; all are good choices. Use only the red, ripe fruits, not the immature green ones. Store them in a closed paper bag in the refrigerator for up to two weeks, or in plastic in the freezer for three months.

THAI CHILIES Thai chilies are only 1½ inches (4 cm) long, but these fiery little specimens pack a lot of heat into their little bodies. Extremely spicy, they can be used both fresh and dried and come in red, green and sometimes orange. When the green immature chilies ripen, they turn red. Keep in a paper bag in the refrigerator for up to two weeks, or freeze them fresh and they should keep well for up to three months. Arbol or Serrano chilies can be substituted if chilies are unavailable.

FROM TOP TO BOTTOM: Long red chillies, Thai chillies, dried chillies.

Asian Noodles

Chinese egg noodles

Rice vermicelli

Somen noodles

Cellophane noodles

Soba noodles

Lo mein egg noodles

Medium-width egg noodles

Thin flat rice noodles or sticks (for pho)

Stir-fry rice noodles (for pad Thai)

Pad Thai rice noodles

BUCKWHEAT NOODLES

Thin and brownish in color, soba (the Japanese name) is made from buckwheat flour, often with wheat flour added. Buckwheat is not a true cereal grain, but is related to rhubarb and sorrel, making it suitable for those who are gluten-free. Buckwheat-only noodles are available—just read the labels. A striking green noodle called *cha soba* is made with green tea. Although soba noodles are often served cold with a dipping sauce (page 88), they can be used interchangeably in any udon recipe. Korean buckwheat noodles (page 113) are chewier in texture, and may also contain sweet potato flour or arrowroot. Soba noodles are usually available dried in the U.S.

CHINESE EGG NOODLES

come in various widths and diameters, and are available fresh or dried. I stock up on both thin and flat dried noodles.

They should be pale yellow in color—bright golden-yellow noodles usually contain food coloring. After a quick boil, I'll use them in stir-fried noodles or toss them with peanut sauce for a quick noodle salad. Fresh uncooked noodles can keep in the refrigerator for about a week. You can also freeze them for about three months. Don't thaw them before using, or they will turn soggy; simply boil them for a little longer than directed on the package. Thin spaghetti makes an acceptable substitute.

CELLOPHANE NOODLES

Made from mung bean starch (hence their other moniker, bean thread noodles), these translucent noodles have a smooth and slippery texture, making them perfect for soup-noodle dishes (page 126). Cellophane noodles are commonly sold dried in packages containing eight to ten bundles, each ranging from 1.3 to 2 ounces

(40 to 60 g). Look for a brand that contains only mung beans and water, with no additives.

FINE RICE NOODLES This

variety, called vermicelli or *maifun*, is great for stir-frying. Deep-frying turns them into a crunchy garnish or a bed for sauces.

MEDIUM PAD THAI NOODLES

Versatile noodles about ¼ inch (6 mm) wide, these can be used in soups, stir-fries, salads—and, of course, for Pad Thai (page 66). Find them in the Asian/international aisle of your local grocery store.

RICE STICKS are flat noodles

made from rice and water—they contain neither mung beans nor wheat. Extremely popular in Southeast Asia, rice sticks come in several different shapes and sizes, which can be roughly classified into thin/small, medium and wide categories. They are most often

available in packages containing 14 or 16 ounces (400 or 450 g) of noodles. Don't worry too much about the size and shape for the recipes in this book.

ROUND RICE NOODLES (*BÚN*)

come in various sizes ranging from small to extra-large. Small round rice noodles are used for Vietnamese Noodle Salad Bowls (page 62). They bear a very close resemblance to rice vermicelli; place the two side by side, however, and you'll be able to tell that rice vermicelli noodles are thinner. These noodles are sold dried as wiry flat skeins or straight sticks in clear plastic packages.

THIN *BANH PHO* NOODLES

These noodles are ⅛ inch (3 mm) or less in width, and are most often used in soups, especially the popular Vietnamese soup-noodle dish pho (page 136). Sometimes they can be found fresh in the refrigerated section of Asian markets.

Asian Herbs

Cilantro (coriander leaves), lemongrass, Asian (kaffir) lime leaf and Thai basil are my favorite Asian herbs. While cilantro is easy to find, lemongrass, lime leaves and Thai basil are usually only available at Asian markets. However, I have seen lemongrass and lime leaves sold fresh and dried at specialty markets like Whole Foods in cities with large Asian populations. If you do have to make a trek to an Asian market to purchase them, take heart: all these herbs (except cilantro) freeze well—as do chilies. You can store them in the freezer for three to six months and they'll still be full of flavor. Just run them under hot water before using, or simply drop them into your soup or stew straight from the freezer. This means you'll only have to make that trek once every few months and you can still cook your favorite Asian dishes in the meantime.

Another solution is to grow Asian herbs at home. They can be easily cultivated in the garden or in containers, according to Wendy Kiang-Spray, master gardener and author of *The Chinese Kitchen Garden: Growing Techniques and Family Recipes from a Classic Cuisine* (Timber Press). She gives some growing tips below.

CLOCKWISE, FROM TOP LEFT: Thai basil, Asian (kaffir) lime leaves, lemongrass stalks, coriander leaves (cilantro)

ASIAN LIME LEAVES (KAFFIR, *MARKUT*) These glossy forest-green leaves are wonderfully aromatic. Crumple them before adding to coconut-milk dishes, soups and braises for a citrusy, floral undertone. The unmistakable double-barrel leaves are best when fresh or frozen. Don't buy dried leaves if you can help it, as they lack aroma and flavor. Asian lime leaves keep for ten days in the refrigerator and up to six months in a zip-top bag in the freezer. If you can't find them, try substituting lime zest, lemon thyme, lemon verbena or lemon myrtle. If you live in a tropical climate, you can plant Asian lime trees in your garden. In other climates, grow them in containers and bring indoors during winter to protect from frost. Lime trees enjoy indoor temperatures around 60°F (16°C) or above, especially during winter months. Prune while young to encourage branching and a bushier plant.

CILANTRO (CORIANDER LEAF, CHINESE PARSLEY) is used to flavor marinades and is also added to noodles, soups and stir-fries as a garnish right before serving. The flavorful, earthy-tasting stems and roots are minced and thrown into curry pastes and stocks. Look for whole cilantro plants with roots at farmer's markets. To grow, buy starter plants or start from seed. To harvest fresh cilantro all season, sow seeds every two to three weeks for a continuous crop. As soon as plants are 3 to 4 inches tall with cuttable leaves, snip them for cooking. Cilantro is an annual and will need to be replenished when mature.

LEMONGRASS These yellowish-green stalks have stiff, lance-like leaves and impart a delicate citrus flavor to soups, curries, and stir-fries. Choose plump stalks that are firm and tight with no signs of mildew or rot. Wrap fresh lemongrass in moist paper towels and store in the refrigerator for up to two weeks. Or freeze them in a zip-top bag for three months. Lemongrass is available dried (at many spice shops), minced (in the freezer section of Asian markets), and as a paste (in the refrigerated produce section of mainstream grocery stores), but ultimately fresh tastes the best. Lemon verbena has a similar flavor. The easiest, cheapest and most rewarding way to start lemongrass is by taking a cutting

from a friend or by finding find fresh green stalks at an Asian supermarket. Place healthy stalks in a glass of water. Change the water every other day or whenever it begins to look murky. Roots should appear within two weeks. When the roots are a couple of inches long and there is no danger of frost, the lemongrass stalks can be planted directly in the garden. Lemongrass can grow to at least three feet tall. Harvest as needed by cutting larger outer stalks at soil level.

Trimming lemongrass: Peel away the loose outer layers. Trim about 1 inch (2.5 cm) from the hard root and cut off the woody top where green meets pale yellow, leaving 3 to 4 inches (7.5 to 10 cm) of the tender white core. Bruise the stem to release the aroma and oils. Throw it whole into soups and stews.

To mince for stir-fries and pastes, slice the stem crosswise into the thinnest ringlets you can cut. Then rock your blade over the slices to chop them into confetti-sized chips. You'll get 1½ to 2 tablespoons of minced lemongrass for every stalk.

THAI BASIL The leaves of Thai basil are smaller and more pointed than those of the Italian sweet basil commonly used to make pesto. The burgundy stems are also a dead giveaway. Its flavor, much like licorice, is distinctive in curries and stir-fries. A mix of Italian basil and mint may be used as a substitute. To grow, start seeds indoors in early spring. Place about three seeds in a small pot; when they germinate, leave the strongest seedling and snip the others at the soil line. Water gently and grow on a sunny windowsill or under grow lights. When plants are about 4 to 6 inches (10 to 15 cm) tall and the soil outside is warm, transplant into the garden. Harvest regularly by cutting stems down to the second set of leaves. This encourages the growth of healthy, full, bushy basil plants.

tute. Because I don't have room for three different types types of cooking spirits, I also use it in recipes that call for mirin (adding a little sugar, because mirin is sweet) or sake.

COCONUT PALM SUGAR

I used to buy palm sugar in disks or cylinders from the Asian market, and it was a bit of a chore to prepare, because pieces have to be shaved off before measuring and throwing

into dishes. Then I discovered granulated coconut palm sugar, and now I'm hooked! It's so much easier to use, and I've seen it at just about every grocery store I've been to. Light or dark brown sugar may be used as a substitute in a pinch, but they don't carry the same complexity of flavor as palm sugar. Keep in mind that brown sugar is sweeter than coconut sugar, so always start off with less than the recipe calls for. Wholesome is a good brand, but even a generic grocery-store brand tastes fine.

CORIANDER SEEDS There are

two types of coriander seeds; the tiny round tan ones with a lemony taste are most common. Like all spices, they are best when used whole. The green coriander leaf is what we

Mae Ploy, Lobo and Aroy-D curry pastes are available at Asian markets, while the Thai Kitchen brand can be found in the Asian aisle of most grocery stores.

CURRY PASTES are a moist blend of ground or pounded herbs and/or spices. Thai curry pastes comprise fresh aromatics such as lemongrass, galangal and chilies that are pounded together into a paste. Red curry paste may also include red chilies, shallots, coriander root, shrimp paste and lime leaves. I applaud you if you want to make curry paste at home; it yields the best flavor and you can control what goes into it (especially if you want to omit shrimp paste and additives). But if you don't want to be hunting down a laundry list of ingredients, a store-bought curry paste such as the vegan Thai Kitchen brand works well and is available in the Asian/international aisle of most grocery stores. Note that not all brands are vegan, so be sure to read the labels!

call cilantro in the U.S. Store coriander seeds in a tightly sealed jar for up to six months.

COCONUT MILK is the creamy, sweet liquid pressed from the freshly grated flesh of mature brown coconuts. I always have a few cans sitting in my pantry for the times I want to whip up a curry or make a sticky rice treat. I buy Chaokoh brand whenever possible. Before opening, always shake the can to mix the richer coconut cream that rises to the top with the thin milk below. Be aware that the large tetra-pak box you may find in the grocery store's refrigerated section isn't suitable for Asian recipes.

wrappers will stay fresh in the refrigerator for up to a week, or in the freezer for up to two months.

DUMPLING WRAPPERS These wrappers, usually made with egg and wheat flour, are available fresh and frozen in square or round shapes and various thicknesses. They can be fried, boiled, steamed or even baked, resulting in different textures: crispy, springy, chewy, or soft as clouds. Dumpling wrappers are usually labeled to indicate their use: wontons, potstickers, siu mai or gyoza. Dumpling

GALANGAL has an earthy aroma and a pine-like flavor with a faint hint of citrus; it is somewhat medicinal. As one of Southeast Asia's most popular aromatics, it is tossed into curries, soups and stews, as well as sambals and sauces. Be sure to remove it before serving, as it has a hard, chewy texture. Wrapped well, the roots will stay fresh in the refrigerator for up to three weeks, or frozen

Korean red pepper paste (*gochujang*) is available in bottles or big tubs.

Ssam-jang or *ssam* sauce (left) is a mixture of fermented bean paste and red pepper paste. It accompanies grilled meats wrapped in lettuce.

KOREAN RED PEPPER PASTE (*GOCHUJANG*) is made from fermented soybeans, glutinous rice, red peppers and malt. Read the labels and buy a brand without additives, especially MSG. Better yet, make your own (page 34). Store it in the refrigerator once opened and it will stay fresh indefinitely.

KOREAN RED PEPPER POWDER (*GOCHUGARU*) Made from hot Korean red peppers, this powder is a brilliant flaming red with a smoky, sweet smell. Some stores offer three grades of the powder. The fine-ground type is used for cooking and making Korean red pepper paste, coarse-ground is for making kimchi, and crushed flakes are for cooking and as a garnish. Store in a tightly covered jar or plastic bag in the refrigerator where it will stay fresh for several months. Most Asian stores carry gochugaru, but if you can't find it, make your own blend. I suggest 2 parts ground paprika powder, 2 parts ground ancho chili powder and 1 part cayenne or generic chili flakes. You'll get a combination of sweet (paprika), smoky (ancho), and spicy hot (cayenne).

Korean red pepper powder is available coarse (for kimchi-making) or fine (to make gochujang).

for up to six months. Galangal is available dried or ground (not bad, if used sparingly), but fresh has lots more flavor. Many recipes suggest ginger as a substitute, but I think the flavors are oceans apart! You'll find galangal in the refrigerated section at Asian markets.

GINGER One of the most versatile and widely used ingredients in Asian cooking, fresh ginger has a warm, zesty flavor and fragrance that adds a spicy bite to both sweet and savory dishes. It is used smashed, grated, sliced, chopped, shredded and juiced. Look for firm, wrinkle-free rhizomes with glossy tan skin. Wrap ginger in paper towels, cover with a plastic bag and refrigerate. In my recipes, "chubby" refers to fresh ginger pieces that are about 1 inch (2.5 cm) in diameter.

KOMBU (KELP) SEAWEED The Japanese name for kelp, kombu is a dark-green—almost black—seaweed with a sweet, ocean-fresh scent. It is sold dried in 1/8 -inch (3-mm)-thick pliable sheets about 10 by 5 inches (25 by 12.5 cm) in size. Kombu is used to make Dashi (page 29). Choose sheets that are very dark and wipe them to remove any grit, but don't rub off the white residue—this is not only safe to eat, but actually incredibly flavorful. Stored in a cool, dark place, kombu keeps indefinitely. Icelandic dulse seaweed is a good substitute if your grocery store doesn't carry kombu in the Asian/international aisle.

MIRIN is a pale-gold spirit used in Japanese cooking to add subtle sweetness to salad dressings, marinades and stews. It was originally a sugar substitute during a time when sugar was scarce and expensive. Look for *hon-mirin* (true mirin), a naturally brewed elixir containing natural sugars; avoid *aji-mirin* or any bottle labeled "sweet cooking seasoning." Opened bottles of mirin can be left on the shelf. I've seen recipes where sugar is used as a mirin substitute (how things change!), but I mix 1/4 cup dry sherry with 2 teaspoons granulated sugar.

MISO is a thick, rich paste made from fermenting rice, barley or soybeans. This flavorful paste is very similar to Chinese *doubanji-ang* and Singapore *taucheo*—they are all made from fermented beans (soybeans, broad beans or lima beans). I keep a big tub of (usually white) miso in my fridge, and use it in recipes calling for these other pastes

RICE We're a family of rice-eaters—I usually buy fragrant white jasmine rice by the 25-pound bag. For the sake of variety I sometimes make brown jasmine rice, which I buy in smaller 1- or 2-pound bags or from the bulk bins. Jasmine rice is an all-purpose type that goes with just about everything we eat. When I can, I buy Elephant or Royal Umbrella brands. I also keep a small bag of Japanese sticky rice or sushi rice on hand. The stickier texture is better suited for making sushi and other Japanese-style dishes. I recommend the Kokuho Rose and Nishiki brands, which are grown in California.

too. There are various grades, colors and strengths, but the two most common are white miso (*shiro-miso*), a mild, sweet miso; and red miso (*aka-miso*) which has a higher salt content and an earthier flavor.

NORI SEAWEED Most familiar as the wrapper for sushi rolls, nori comes in crisp, thin sheets pre-cut for this purpose, and ranges in color from a dark green to a deep purple. It is used not only to wrap sushi, but also as a garnish for soups. Keep nori in a cool, dark place, and store it wrapped up in plastic if possible. For a fun change, I like to substitute Kale "Chips" (page 26) over soups.

PANKO Panko are coarse breadcrumbs used in Japanese cuisine to coat deep-fried foods like tempura and *tonkatsu*. They can be found in the Asian/international section of most grocery stores in cellophane packages or canisters. The unopened packages last indefinitely. Once opened, panko should be frozen.

POTATO STARCH is the gold standard for making perfect Japanese *kara-age* (fried chicken), as it produces a light, crispy coating. While cornstarch is usually the thickener of choice in Chinese cooking, cornstarch and potato starch can be used interchangeably in both instances. Mix 1 part starch with 2 or 3 parts water to make a slurry. Bob's Red Mill sells potato starch in 24-ounce (680-g) bags that are available at many grocery stores.

PRESERVED RADISH, sometimes labeled salted radish, comes in both salty and sweet versions. While sweet is prefer-able for pad Thai, preserved radish is generally not very easy to come by, so just buy what you can find—sweet or salty, finely chopped, whole or in long strips.

RICE FLOUR, usually made from long-grain rice, is the basis of rice noodles. It's also used for making sweets in Malaysia and Indonesia. Until just a few years ago, rice flour was only sold at Asian markets, but due to the high demand for gluten-free products, brands like Bob's Red Mill now offer rice flour in 24-ounce (720-g) packages through mainstream grocery stores.

SESAME OIL This thick, amber-colored oil is pressed from toasted sesame seeds. I use it as a seasoning, not a cooking oil—I like to drizzle it over stir-fries and soups and add it to marinades.

SESAME SEEDS My pantry is stocked with both white and black sesame seeds for sprinkling over salads and into dipping sauces. I also like to grind them into a paste for making noodle sauces and sweets. Toasting brings out their nutty flavor. They're available already toasted but you can do it at home, too (page 25).

Black and white sesame seeds. If possible, buy toasted seeds.

Darker sesame oil has stronger flavor. I use Kadoya brand.

TAMARIND is a popular souring agent in Southeast Asian cooking, with a more complex flavor than lime or lemon. You probably know it as a key flavoring in pad Thai (see Tamarind Sweet and Sour Sauce, page 67), but its uses extend much further, to soups and stir-fries. I always buy "wet tamarind"—the sticky, coffee-colored pulp is pressed into semi-pliable blocks and packaged in cellophane. The pulp must be soaked in hot water to form a paste before using. Tamarind concentrate—processed pulp in a cylindrical container—is convenient, but the flavor cannot compare. In a cool, dry place, blocks of tamarind last almost forever! Substitute lime juice if you must.

Seedless "wet tamarind" comes in clear cellophane packages, and is sold at Asian markets.

RICE VINEGAR The 24-ounce (710-ml) bottle I buy goes quickly! I use rice vinegar for pickling, in dressings and in dipping sauces; a few drizzles will punch up any dish with a mellow acidic flavor. In a pinch, cider vinegar is a good substitute. Try to avoid using white distilled vinegar, as it's much sharper. If you have no alternative, use less than what the recipes calls for.

SALT, PEPPER AND SUGAR I buy fine sea salt because it is less processed than iodized table salt and has a more complex flavor. Plus, if you make fermented products like kimchi, as well as pickles, the additives in table salt may interfere with the fermentation process and/ or cause the brine to go cloudy.

Don't be mistaken, though—they both contain the same amount of sodium.

Although ground white pepper powder is more commonly used in Asia, I use black peppercorns, grinding them directly into my cooking. White pepper is just husked black peppercorns anyway, so which one you use is just a matter of preference.

Organic raw cane sugar is my preferred sugar. Eco-friendly and unrefined, it has the full-bodied taste of sugarcane and undergoes less processing than white sugar.

SAMBAL OELEK Chili paste, or *sambal* in Malay or Indonesian, is a popular condiment in Southeast Asian cuisine; it conveniently comes in a bottle. Indonesian *sambal oelek* is my favorite. Named for the grinding or pounding action used to make it in a mortar, *sambal oelek* comprises a mixture of fresh chilies, vinegar and salt. This fiery mixture results in a powerful flavor that complements almost any dish (see page 32). Kept in your refrigerator, *sambal oelek* will last indefinitely.

SICHUAN PEPPERCORNS Sichuan peppercorns may resemble black peppercorns, but they are actually berries. They have a spicy, slightly woodsy flavor and leave a numbing sensation on the tongue. Before using, toast them in a skillet and crush them. To preserve their flavor, keep them in an airtight jar in a cool place. An intensely flavored peppercorn like Tellicherry is a good substitute.

SOY SAUCE There are many different varieties of this condiment, which is made from fermented roasted soybeans and ground wheat. Sometimes I'll stock both a Japanese-style and a Chinese-style soy sauce in my pantry. Japanese soy sauce (*shoyu*) contains more wheat (Japanese tamari, however, contains little to none) and is darker and less salty than the Chinese variety. Most of the time, I'll have just one or the other. You can hardly taste the difference in a cooked dish. Kikkoman and Pearl River Bridge make good soy sauces across the board.

SPRING ROLL WRAPPERS are thin sheets of dough that range in size from 4 to 8 inches (10 to 20 cm) square. I prefer these to the thick wrappers usually used for fried egg rolls served at Chinese restaurants in the U.S. Spring roll wrappers can be used for Indonesian, Vietnamese, and Filipino versions of fried spring rolls. Choose paper-thin, translucent wrappers like the Spring Home brand, found in the refrigerated section at Asian markets.

Store dumpling and spring roll wrappers in the refrigerator or freezer, but let them come to room temperature before using. While assembling, cover the stack of wrappers with a damp cloth to keep them moist. The wrappers are very delicate and prone to tearing. If possible, buy the ones that are already separated, and always buy extra!

SRIRACHA HOT CHILI SAUCE In the U.S., sriracha is synonymous with Huy Fong Foods. The California-based company makes the sauce from chili peppers, distilled vinegar, garlic, sugar and salt. Their signature squeeze bottles with the green cap and a rooster on the front are a fixture on tabletops across the country.

STAR ANISE These eight-pronged star-shaped pods impart an intense licorice flavor and fragrance to braises and soups. Hard and reddish-brown, star anise is usually sold in plastic bags; it should be stored in an airtight jar away from light and heat. Both star anise and aniseed contain the essential oil anethole, and one can be substituted for the other.

STICKY RICE Also called glutinous rice, it comes in two colors—white and purple. White sticky rice—which is not to be confused with Japanese sushi rice—turns from opaque to translucent and clumps together once it's cooked. Whole-grain purple sticky rice has a sweet, nutty taste and is commonly used for mak-

TOFU is a high-protein, low-fat wonder that is made by coagulating fresh soy milk with a calcium compound to form curds, which are then pressed together into cakes. Tofu comes in several varieties, ranging from silky-soft and fragile to firm and dense. The type you use will depend on your cooking method, and sometimes your taste. House, Sunrise and Sun Luck are good brands available at many markets, both specialty and mainstream.

Delicate **silken tofu** is only suitable for soups, braises and desserts. Don't try to deep-fry silken tofu, as it can react dangerously with hot oil.

Medium-firm (*momen*) tofu can be battered, baked, boiled or braised.

Firm or extra-firm tofu can be sliced, diced and cubed; it is sturdy enough for stir-fries and deep-frying. Extra-firm is drier and not as silky in texture.

DRAINING TOFU Tofu should always be drained—or at least blotted— before using, especially when deep-frying. Cover a cutting board or rimmed plate with two layers of paper towels or non-terry kitchen towels. Place the tofu on top and cover the tofu with two layers of fresh towels. Carefully place a heavy weight, such as a book or pot, on the tofu. Drain for 15 minutes, changing the towels as needed.

Firm and medium tofu are the most versatile types.

ing desserts. Both types are usually found only at Asian markets. If you can't find white sticky rice, use purple.

TURMERIC imbues dishes with a peppery, musky flavor. The fresh rhizome has a rich orange tint and a gingery taste that is lacking in the ground dried form. However, the recipes in this book call for only the powdered version. Look for turmeric powder that is a pure deep yellow or gold. Store in an airtight container.

VEGETABLE OIL With their neutral flavor and high smoke point, vegetable oils (corn, peanut, safflower, soybean, sunflower) are the best choices for Asian cooking. I generally use organic cold-pressed sunflower oil. Feel free to use your choice of oil, but note that different oils add slightly different flavors to your dishes. It's best to experiment with a variety of oils for different purposes.

Basic Recipes

In this chapter, you'll find all the basic recipes I use to amp up flavors and add dimension to my Asian vegetarian cooking. Highlights include how to cook rice on the stovetop, garnishes to add flavor and texture, and stocks for stir-fries and soups. I also give recipes for homemade versions of prepared sauces and spice mixes that are easy to whip up at home. And don't forget pickles and fermented vegetables that make delicious snacks or meal accompaniments!

Stovetop Jasmine Rice

Fragrant jasmine is my rice of choice for pairing with most dishes. Cooking rice in a pot can be tricky, depending on the type of rice you're cooking as well as how old the rice is. The only foolproof way to perfect that pot of rice is to cook several batches from the same bag of rice and experiment. If the rice is too dry, add more water a few tablespoons at a time. If it's too soggy, decrease the water bit by bit. This recipe is for white rice, but you can use the same method to cook brown jasmine rice, as well as other types of medium- to long-grain rice. See "Tips" below and check package directions for the correct rice-to-water ratios.

PREP TIME: 5 MINUTES
COOK TIME: 40 MINUTES
MAKES: ABOUT 2 CUPS

1 cup (200 g) jasmine rice
1¼ cups (325 ml) water

In a medium heavy-bottomed saucepan with a tight-fitting lid (preferably glass so you can observe cooking), rinse the rice in at least 3 changes of water. Drain well.

Add the 1¼ cups (325 ml) water and swirl the rice with your hand. Let the grains settle evenly at the bottom of saucepan.

Set the saucepan on the stove over high heat and bring to a rolling boil, so that the water is bubbling around the circumference of the saucepan. Reduce the heat to the lowest possible setting and cover the

saucepan tightly with the lid. Continue cooking for 15 to 18 minutes, or until all the water is absorbed. The rice will look moist, and the contents will still be bubbling. Turn off the heat and let rice steam, lid intact, for another 10 minutes. Then lift off the lid and gently fluff the rice with a fork or a pair of chopsticks. The rice should not be lumpy; the individual grains should be separate.

Keep rice covered until ready to serve. Serve hot.

Tips Visit smithsonianapa.org/picklesandtea/how-to-cook-rice-3-ways/ for other methods of cooking rice.
• To cook Japanese rice in a clay pot, visit: smithsonianapa.org/picklesandtea/the-ritual-of-rice/
• To make brown rice, use a 1:2 ratio of rice to water and cook for at least 30 minutes.

Toasted Sesame Seeds

Toasting sesame seeds helps bring out their rich aroma and nutty taste.

PREP TIME: 5 MINUTES
MAKES: ¼ CUP (30 G)

¼ cup (30 g) white sesame seeds

Preheat a medium nonstick cast-iron skillet over high heat for 2 to 3 minutes until wisps of smoke start to appear. Reduce the heat to medium-low and add the sesame seeds, spreading them out in one layer. Toast for 2 to 4 minutes, stirring or shaking the pan often, until the seeds are aromatic and begin to brown and pop. Allow to cool before using or storing.

Microwaved Crispy Garlic Bits

Fried garlic is usually prepared on the stove, but using a microwave is far more convenient when making the small quantities normally used in the home kitchen. You can also buy fried garlic in round canisters at an Asian market, but you'll miss out on the flavorful garlic oil.

PREP TIME: 4 MINUTES
COOK TIME: 1 MINUTE
MAKES: 2 TABLESPOONS

2 tablespoons minced garlic (about 6 cloves)
Vegetable oil

Place the garlic in a small microwavable bowl that is large enough to prevent overflow.

   Add just enough oil to cover the garlic. Microwave on high for 1 to 2 minutes, checking every 30 seconds to see if it's done. Remove the garlic when it's light brown, as it will continue to cook in the hot oil after it is taken out of the microwave. The bits should be golden brown when cool. Drain the garlic in a fine-mesh sieve over a bowl, reserving the garlic oil for another use. Store the garlic bits in an airtight container for 2 to 3 days.

Toasted Coconut Flakes

You may be more accustomed to using coconut flakes in baking, but they're a very tasty addition to many savory Asian dishes. I prefer big unsweetened coconut flakes to shredded coconut, which burns very quickly. If you have time and inclination, go with the oven method. The flakes will toast more evenly and come out crunchier.

COOK TIME: 10 MINUTES
MAKES: 1 CUP (60 G)

1 cup (60 g) unsweetened large-flake coconut

OVEN METHOD:

Preheat oven to 325°F (160°C). Spread the coconut flakes out evenly in one layer on a rimmed baking sheet. Bake for 8 to 10 minutes, stirring occasionally, until they turn golden brown. Remove from the oven and transfer to a large plate to cool. Don't leave the coconut on the baking sheet because it will continue to brown.

STOVETOP METHOD:

Spread coconut flakes out in a large skillet and set over medium heat. Cook for 3 to 5 minutes, stirring frequently, until the coconut is evenly golden brown.

MICROWAVE OVEN METHOD:

Spread coconut out in a microwave-safe pan. Microwave on high for 4½ to 8 minutes, tossing the coconut with a fork after each minute.

Tip Keep for two weeks in an airtight container.

Kale "Chips"

This recipe has made kale the new darling of the culinary world. I like to use kale chips as a substitute for roasted seaweed (nori) or serve them as a snack. Lacinato kale (also known as dinosaur or Tuscan kale) is my favorite, but any type of kale will do.

PREP TIME: 10 MINUTES
COOK TIME: 20 MINUTES
MAKES: 4 TO 6 SERVINGS

1 bunch (10 oz/300 g) kale, washed and thoroughly
  dried
2 tablespoons vegetable oil
1 teaspoon fine sea salt

Preheat oven to 275°F (135°C).
   Remove ribs from the kale and tear leaves into bite-sized pieces. Place on a greased baking sheet. Drizzle with the oil and sprinkle with the salt, then toss with your hands. Arrange the seasoned leaves in a single layer (use two baking sheets if needed). Bake until crisp, turning the leaves halfway through, about 20 minutes.

Fried Shallots

You can buy fried shallots at an Asian market; even French-fried onions (the kind used for green bean casserole) are okay. They are fantastic sprinkled over just about anything, including burgers and steamed vegetables. But they are tastiest made at home. My mom always fried them in bulk, filling an entire gallon container. The trick is to start in cold oil and cook them slowly. The flavorful cooking oil tastes great in other recipes.

PREP TIME: 5 MINUTES + 1 HOUR STANDING TIME
COOK TIME: 15 MINUTES
MAKES: ¾ CUP

3 large shallots (6 oz/170 g), peeled and
  sliced lengthwise about ⅛ inch (3 mm) thick
Vegetable oil, for frying

Pat the shallots dry with paper towels and let them air-dry on your kitchen counter (or out in the sun like my mom used to do!) for about 1 hour.
   Pour enough oil into a small saucepan to reach a depth of 2 inches (5 cm). Add the shallots and set the saucepan over medium heat. Adjust the heat to keep the oil bubbling gently. Cook, stirring occasionally, for about 15 to 20 minutes, until the shallots turn golden brown. Reduce the heat if they color too quickly.
   Place a fine-meshed sieve over a bowl and drain the shallots, reserving the oil. Cool completely and store in an airtight container for up to one week.

Quick Ramen Eggs

Cooked eggs soaked in sweet soy sauce (*ni-tamago*) is a popular ramen topping. I like my egg yolks gooey, but you can cook them for longer (up to 10 minutes) if you prefer firmer yolks.

PREP TIME: 5 MINUTES
COOK TIME: 8½ MINUTES + 1 HOUR TO MARINATE

4 large eggs
4 tablespoons water
3 tablespoons soy sauce
2 tablespoons mirin or rice vinegar
1 tablespoon granulated sugar

Bring a large pot of water to a rolling boil over high heat. Reduce heat to medium and lower eggs in gently. Cook for 6½ minutes, then plunge into a bowl of ice water to stop the cooking.

While the eggs are cooling, make the marinade. Stir together the water, soy sauce, mirin, and sugar in a small container (the eggs should fit inside snugly) until the sugar dissolves. Microwave for 30 seconds to dissolve sugar, if necessary.

When the eggs are cool, peel them and place them in the container. Turn to coat and place a small dish on top to keep them submerged. Refrigerate for at least 1 hour or (preferably) overnight. Drain and serve.

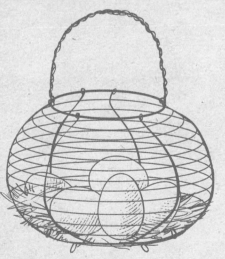

Tempeh Three Ways

Tempeh can be an acquired taste, but it's protein-packed and easy to digest because it's fermented. Before cooking, I recommend simmering sliced tempeh in boiling water for 10 minutes to remove any bitterness. Then drain and proceed with marinating.

PREP TIME: 5 MINUTES + MARINATING TIME
COOK TIME: 5 TO 25 MINUTES

4 tablespoons soy sauce
1 tablespoon rice vinegar (or whatever vinegar you have)
1 tablespoon water
1 teaspoon sesame or vegetable oil
2 cloves garlic, minced
Pinch of granulated sugar
One 8-oz (250-g) package tempeh, cut into ¼-in (5-mm) slices

Mix together the soy sauce, rice vinegar, water, oil, garlic and sugar in a medium bowl. Add the tempeh, turning to coat. Marinate for 20 minutes up to 1 hour.

Pan-fry in an oiled skillet over medium heat until golden brown and crispy, 1 to 1½ minutes on each side.

Alternately, grill over medium heat until lightly charred, 1 to 2 minutes on each side.

Or bake at 375°F (190°C) for 12 to 15 minutes, then turn over and bake for another 10 minutes.

Roasted Veggie Stock

Cutting the vegetables into small pieces (the finer the dice the better) extracts greater flavor; roasting caramelizes and makes the flavors more complex. If you have time for additional simmering, do so. The vegetables suggested below are just a guide. Use 8 to 9 cups (450 to 500 g) of any chopped veggies you have on hand. Be aware that starchy ones like potatoes can make your stock cloudy. Strong-flavored vegetables like cabbage and broccoli may overpower your stock, but that can be a good thing if it suits your taste.

PREP TIME: 20 MINUTES
COOK TIME: 2 HOURS

2 tablespoons vegetable oil, divided
4 large carrots, sliced
3 celery stalks, chopped
1 large yellow onion, quartered and
   left unpeeled
1 large leek, greens and whites, chopped
1 daikon radish or large purple turnip,
   chopped
10 white or brown button mushrooms,
   sliced
6 cloves garlic, smashed
12 cups (3 liters) water
Chubby 2-in (5-cm) knob fresh ginger,
   sliced along the grain
1 small bunch cilantro stems or stems
   with leaves, tied with kitchen twine
   (about 15 stems)
¼ cup (60 ml) soy sauce (optional)
Fine sea salt

Preheat oven to 425°F (220°C).

Line two rimmed baking sheets with foil and spray with cooking spray. Divide the vegetables equally between the sheets and spread them out in a single layer. Drizzle each baking sheet with 1 tablespoon oil and toss vegetables to coat. Roast for 45 minutes to 1 hour, until well browned. Set aside.

Combine the water, ginger and cilantro in a medium stockpot. Add the roasted vegetables and bring to a boil over high heat. Reduce heat so the stock bubbles steadily but gently. Simmer until the vegetables are very tender, at least 1 hour, or up to 2 or 3 hours if you have the time.

Strain, then add the soy sauce, if using (omit if using in a recipe that calls for low-sodium stock). Taste and adjust seasonings, adding more soy sauce or salt, before using or storing. The stock will keep in the freezer for up to a month.

Tip If you don't have time for roasting, heat the oil in the stock pot, then add the vegetables and let them brown for a few minutes before adding the water.

Dashi Seaweed Stock

Seaweed stock, or dashi, is the basic stock used in Japanese cuisine. It's normally made with both kombu seaweed and dried bonito (skipjack tuna) flakes. You can infuse this vegan version with more umami oomph by adding 4 to 5 dried shiitake stems or 1 large cap to the dashi pot if you can get your hands on some. If you can't find kombu, dulse (a sea vegetable more commonly harvested in the West) is an option too.

PREP TIME: 30 MINUTES

COOK TIME: 5 MINUTES

MAKES: 4 CUPS (1 LITER)

One 3 x 3-in (7.5 x 7.5-cm) square piece of kombu
  or ½ cup (8 g) loosely packed dulse
4 cups (1 liter) filtered water

Combine the kombu or dulse and water in a medium saucepan. Steep for 30 minutes.

Bring the water to a near boil over medium-low heat. This will take 5 to 7 minutes—bubbles will ring the edges of the saucepan. Do not let the dashi boil, or it will turn cloudy and acquire a strong taste of the sea.

Turn off the heat and let cool completely.

Line a fine-mesh sieve with a paper towel or cheesecloth and strain the dashi into a container, reserving the kombu for use in soup. Dashi keeps refrigerated for 3 to 4 days or frozen for up to two months.

NO-COOK METHOD:
Place the kombu in a large glass jar. Pour in the water and cover. Let stand at room temperature for at least 30 minutes and up to 12 hours, or in the refrigerator for at least 8 hours and up to 48 hours. Remove the kombu before use. Keeps refrigerated for 4 to 5 days.

Tip You can also find kelp granules at specialty markets and health-food stores. Use 1 tablespoon in place of the kombu or dulse.

Mushroom Stock

This rich mushroom stock makes a great change from vegetable stock. It's perfect for cooking strong-flavored dishes like Warming Vegetable Pho (page 136). Use any combination of fresh mushrooms you can find. If you're frugally minded, save stems in the freezer every time you cook with mushrooms until you have enough to make this stock. Dried shiitakes or porcinis, with their concentrated flavor, will add dense umami, too. Don't throw away your onion skins either—just pop them into this stock. You'll be straining it anyway.

PREP TIME: 15 MINUTES

COOK TIME: 1 HOUR

MAKES: 10 CUPS (2.5 LITERS)

2 tablespoons vegetable oil
1 lb (500 g) mushrooms, caps and stems both sliced
6 cloves garlic, chopped
2 cups (300 g) roughly chopped yellow onion (save the peels!)
Fine sea salt
12 cups (3 liters) water
8 medjool dates
Peels from chopped onion (above)

Optional Ingredients

¼ cup (7 g) dried mushrooms like porcini or shiitake
Pinch of dried orange peel
Soy sauce to taste (omit if using in a recipe that calls for low-sodium stock)
¼ cup (60 ml) Chinese cooking wine or dry sherry

Add the vegetable oil to a medium stockpot and set over medium-high heat until shimmering hot. Add the mushrooms, garlic and onion, plus a pinch of salt. Stir and cook until the mushrooms release their juices, 4 to 6 minutes.

Pour in the water, then add the dates, dried mushrooms (if using), onion peels and optional dried orange peel. Bring to a boil, then reduce heat until bubbling gently. Cover and simmer for at least 1 hour (2 hours is even better).

Add the soy sauce and cooking wine, if using. Taste and adjust seasonings as needed. Strain stock through a fine-mesh sieve into a heatproof bowl. Refrigerate for up to 4 days or freeze for a month.

Homemade Vegetable Bouillon

Several years ago, I found dehydrated vegetable-stock granules at the Asian market. I was very intrigued; I liked the idea of having bouillon on hand for making a quick vegetable stock or flavoring a stir-fry. So when Heidi Swanson first published her bouillon recipe (adapted from *The River Cottage Preserves Handbook* by Pam Corbin) on her blog, "101 Cookbooks," I got very excited. To "Asian-ify" the recipe, I added vegetables and herbs with flavor profiles you'd normally find in Asian dishes. But you could use any vegetables that you have in your refrigerator. Roughly chop them into pieces that will fit into your food processor.

PREP TIME: 30 MINUTES
MAKES: 3 CUPS (ABOUT 220 G)

3 medium garlic cloves, peeled
Chubby 2-in (5-cm) knob fresh ginger,
    peeled and sliced
2 medium shallots, peeled and chopped
2 small leeks with the green tops chopped
    off, halved and soaked in water to remove
    grit, then sliced crosswise
2 large carrots, chopped
2 large celery stalks with leaves, chopped
½ small head cabbage, chopped
½ small fennel bulb, chopped
½ cup (150 g) fine sea salt
1 small bunch cilantro stems and leaves
    (coriander), roughly chopped
10 green onions (scallions), white and
    green parts, chopped

Place the garlic, ginger, shallots and leeks in a food processor and pulse about 20 times. Add the carrots, celery, cabbage and fennel, and pulse a few more times. Add the salt and pulse 4 or 5 times. Then add the cilantro and green onions and pulse until a coarse, loose paste like wet sand forms. You may have to stir everything up a few times so that all the vegetables and herbs are chopped and fully integrated. I recommend starting with 1 teaspoon bouillon per cup (250 ml) water, but feel free to adjust this ratio according to your palate.

Tips This recipe requires a food processor that holds at least 8 cups (2 liters).
• Keep the bouillon in a sealed container in the freezer. You'll be able to scoop it out without defrosting because of the salt.
• You can freeze the purée in ice-cube trays—then you'll have true bouillon cubes!
• If you don't like the bits of vegetable that end up floating around in your soup, scoop the bouillon into a reusable tea or spice bag and steep to use.

Five-Spice Powder

Five-spice powder is a blend that includes star anise and cinnamon, as well as any combination of cloves, fennel, ginger, nutmeg and Sichuan peppercorn. This pungent spice combination is a wonderful flavor enhancer for stews, barbecued pork and even desserts. If you compare ingredients in different brands of store-bought five-spice powder, you'll see that there are always five different spices, but they're never identical. The key is to balance five flavors: salty, sour, bitter, pungent and sweet.

COOK TIME: 5 MINUTES
MAKES: ¼ CUP (20 G)

6 whole star anise pods, broken into small pieces
One 3-in (7.5-cm) cinnamon or cassia stick,
  broken into small pieces
1 tablespoon Sichuan peppercorns or
  flavorful black peppercorns like Tellicherry
1 tablespoon fennel seeds
2 teaspoons whole cloves

Preheat a medium nonstick or cast-iron skillet over high heat for 2 to 3 minutes, until you see wisps of smoke. Reduce the heat to medium and add the star anise and cinnamon. Toast, stirring occasionally with a wooden spoon, for about 1 minute. Add the Sichuan peppercorns, fennel and cloves. Stir or shake the pan constantly to keep the spices moving. Let them darken and even smoke a little. If they darken too quickly and start to burn, reduce the heat. When they start to pop and smell fragrant, 2 to 4 minutes more, remove from the heat. Allow to cool completely, then grind into a powder with a spice grinder or mortar and pestle.

   Store in an airtight container away from direct sunlight for up to 6 months.

Tips If you have ground spice powders, by all means use them. Just combine in similar (or dissimilar, according to your taste) ratios to those above.
  • Ground aniseed powder can be used in place of star anise; 1 stick cinnamon is equal to about ½ teaspoon ground cinnamon powder.

Yellow Curry Powder

Southeast Asian cooks use a yellow curry powder similar to Madras curry powder. I use whole spices whenever possible, because they keep their flavor better. Because it's not always easy to find whole spices, however, I've given ground equivalents. Whole spices and ground powders aren't used in the same quantities. If you use spice powders, just stir to combine— there's no need to toast them.

PREP TIME: 10 MINUTES
MAKES: ½ CUP (60 G)

4 small dried chilies (more or fewer to taste),
  shoulders snipped and seeds removed as desired
Two 3-in (7.5-cm) cinnamon sticks (or 1 teaspoon
  ground powder)
3 teaspoons coriander seeds (or 2¼ teaspoons
  ground powder)
2 teaspoon cumin seeds (or 1½ teaspoons ground
  powder)
1 teaspoon fennel seeds (or ¾ teaspoon ground
  powder)
4 whole cloves (or ¼ teaspoon ground powder)
1 teaspoon ground nutmeg powder
3 tablespoons ground turmeric powder

Preheat a medium nonstick or cast-iron skillet for 2 to 3 minutes over high heat until you see wisps of smoke. Reduce the heat to medium and add the dried chilies and cinnamon sticks. Toast for about 1 minute, stirring occasionally with a wooden spoon. Add the smaller whole spices—coriander, cumin, fennel, and cloves—and continue toasting until aromatic, another 2 to 4 minutes. Stir or shake the pan constantly to prevent the spices from burning. Remove from the heat and allow to cool completely.

   Place the whole spices in an electric spice/coffee grinder and grind to a powder. Add the nutmeg and turmeric to the grinder and pulse for a few seconds to mix well. Alternately, grind all spices together with a mortar and pestle.

   Store in an airtight container away from direct sunlight. Keeps for up to 6 months.

Homemade Sambal Oelek Chili Paste

Sambal oelek literally means "ground chili paste" in Indonesian. At its most basic, it contains just chilies and salt. If you like it really spicy, add some Thai chilies. The Indonesian name for the long chilies used in this and other *sambal*s or chili pastes is *cabe keriting* (curly chili), but any long red chilies — Fresno, serrano, or whatever chilies are waiting to be picked in your garden before the first frost appears — will do. I've found nice, fat unnamed long chilies about 8 inches (20 cm) long at my local Asian market. A small bowl of *sambal oelek* beside your plate will have you dip-dipping away!

PREP TIME: 10 MINUTES
MAKES: ABOUT ¼ CUP

Two 8-in (18-cm) long red chilies
Fine sea salt
Juice from 1 key lime, or 1 to 2
  teaspoons vinegar
Granulated sugar, to taste (optional)

Stem the chilies and slice them lengthwise. Remove the membrane and seeds as desired (these give chilies their heat).

Chop the chilies up and place in a mortar with a generous pinch of salt. Grind with the pestle, using a twisting motion, until the mixture is pulpy.

Add the lime juice, along with the sugar, if using, and additional salt to taste. Serve immediately.

> *Tip* To make this chili paste in bulk, I strongly advise using a food processor. *Sambal oelek* will keep in a sterilized jar in the fridge for a week.

Homemade Roasted Chili Paste

This dark, flavorful chili sauce is a wonderful accompaniment to many Southeast Asian dishes. Unsurprisingly, each cuisine has its variations— Indonesian cooks like my mom would add tomatoes and/or red bell peppers. Thai cooks may or may not add sugar. The classic version usually contains shrimp paste. You can choose whether or not to fry the paste once it comes together.

PREP TIME: 5 MINUTES
COOK TIME: 10 MINUTES
MAKES: ½ CUP (125 G)

4 fresh long red chilies like Fresno (3 oz/85 g total), stemmed and seeded as desired
1 to 2 Thai chilies (optional)
¼ cup (60 ml) vegetable oil
¼ cup (30 g) garlic, peeled
¼ cup (45 g) shallots, peeled; chopped if they are large
½ teaspoon fine sea salt
1½ teaspoons coconut palm sugar or 1 teaspoon dark brown sugar
2 teaspoons lime juice (½ large lime) or tamarind juice

Preheat a medium nonstick or cast iron skillet over high heat for 2 to 3 minutes until you see wisps of smoke. Reduce the heat to medium and add the red chilies and Thai chilies, if using. Dry-roast for 6 to 8 minutes, turning occasionally, until chilies turn brittle and are lightly charred. Transfer to a plate.

Swirl vegetable oil into a medium skillet and set over medium heat until shimmering hot. Fry the garlic and shallots, turning frequently, until charred on the outside and soft on the inside, 8 to 10 minutes. Transfer them to the same plate as the chilies.

When cool enough to handle, remove the skin and burnt spots from the chilies, garlic and shallots. In a small food processor, grind the chilies until they resemble confetti. Then add the garlic and shallots and grind until a coarse paste forms. Add the salt, sugar and lime or tamarind juice and mix well. Taste and adjust seasonings as needed. If you stop here, the paste will last 2 or 3 days in the refrigerator.

Tip Personal preference is key, so feel free to add seasonings according to your taste.

OPTIONAL STEP:

To make the paste last longer and deepen its flavor, add 2 tablespoons oil to the skillet and fry the finished paste over medium heat for about 2 to 3 minutes until it turns dark and aromatic.

Remove from the heat and use as a condiment or a stir-fry paste. To store, let the paste cool completely before transferring to a glass jar with a tight cap. It will keep refrigerated for up to 2 weeks.

Homemade Korean Hot Pepper Paste

You can buy Korean red hot pepper paste (*gochujang*) at most Asian markets, but it's just as easy to make at home according to your own taste. Traditionally, gochujang is fermented in earthen pots outdoors for months before using, but this easy method, which requires no fermentation, simplifies the process. It's still very tasty, and works well in recipes or as a dip. You can use any type of miso—white, red or brown. In fact, try mixing a couple together for a more complex flavor.

COOK TIME: 10 MINUTES + COOLING TIME
MAKES: ⅔ CUP (200 G)

⅓ cup (85 ml) water
⅓ cup (60 g) dark brown sugar
¼ cup (75 g) white, red or brown miso
¼ cup (25 g) Korean red pepper powder
1 teaspoon soy sauce
½ teaspoon Japanese sake or dry sherry
½ teaspoon rice vinegar

Pour the water into a small saucepan and set over medium-low heat. Add the brown sugar and stir with a wooden spoon until completely dissolved. Add the miso and continuing stirring, pressing out any lumps, until the mixture is smooth, 4 to 6 minutes.

Add the chili pepper powder and keep stirring until the mixture thickens and starts bubbling gently, 2 to 4 minutes. Remove from the heat and cool to room temperature. Add the soy sauce to taste, then stir in the sake and rice vinegar to stop fermentation.

Transfer to a sealed container. May be refrigerated for up to 6 months.

Vegan "Fish" Sauce

Mark Bittman first popularized vegan fish sauce in his cookbook *How to Cook Everything Vegetarian*. Now everyone has their own rendition— including me! Kombu kelp is available at many grocery stores. If you can't find it, look for dulse (kelp flakes).

PREP TIME: 2 MINUTES
COOK TIME: 15 MINUTES
MAKES: ⅓ CUP (85 ML)

One 3 x 3-in (7.5 x 7.5-cm) piece kombu, wiped with a damp cloth, or ¼ cup (4 g) crumbled dulse or other sea vegetable
1 large dried shiitake or other dried mushroom, optional
½ cup (125 ml) soy sauce
1 tablespoon granulated sugar
1 tablespoon lime juice

Place the kombu, dried shiitake (if using), and soy sauce in a small saucepan and set over medium-low heat. Heat until steam rises, but don't allow to boil. Simmer for 10 minutes, then stir in the sugar and lime juice. Simmer for another 5 minutes to allow the flavors to meld, until the sauce has reduced to about ⅓ cup (85 ml).

Strain into a container, pressing out as much liquid as possible. Add 1 to 2 tablespoons water to mellow out the flavor as needed. Refrigerate for up to a month.

Homemade Hoisin Sauce

Hoisin sauce is a popular Chinese seasoning. It's used in stir-fries and also as a marinade or condiment. I love it, but it's hard to find a brand that doesn't contain any additives. Plus, I prefer consuming organic or non-GMO soy products. I haven't been able to find organic hoisin sauce, so I came up with my own recipe using organic miso. I use white miso because that's what I usually buy (I think it's the most versatile), but if you prefer red or brown, feel free to use that instead.

PREP TIME: 5 MINUTES
MAKES: ½ CUP (125 ML)

¼ cup (75 g) miso
½ cup (125 ml) honey
2 tablespoons sesame oil
4 teaspoons rice vinegar
1 teaspoon minced garlic or ¼ teaspoon garlic powder
½ teaspoon Five-Spice Powder (page 31)
1 to 2 teaspoons *sambal oelek* or other chili paste

Combine all ingredients in a bowl and whisk together until smooth. May be refrigerated for up to 6 months in a sealed container.

Tip To make vegan, use maple syrup or agave syrup instead of honey.

Gourmet Indonesian Peanut Sauce

The title says it all. This is based on my mom's recipe, which accompanies Mixed Vegetable Salad with Indonesian Peanut Sauce (page 81). Raw peanuts are roasted on the stovetop or in the oven, and then ground. You'll also have to hunt down tamarind pulp and lime leaves, but it's worth the trouble— the addition of freshly roasted peanuts and fragrant herbs makes for unsurpassed flavor.

PREP TIME: 5 MINUTES
COOK TIME: 25 MINUTES
MAKES: 1 CUP (250 ML)

2 tablespoons vegetable oil (or just
  enough to coat the peanuts)
1 cup plus 2 tablespoons (200 g) raw
  skinless peanuts
1½ cups (375 ml) water
2 Asian (*kaffir*) lime leaves (optional)
1 tablespoon seedless wet tamarind
  pulp, or 2 tablespoons freshly squeezed
  lime juice
3 tablespoons coconut palm sugar
  or 2 tablespoons dark brown sugar
2 teaspoons fine sea salt
1 teaspoon *sambal oelek* chili *paste*
1 to 2 Thai chilies, chopped (optional)

Tips Raw peanuts—skin-on and skinless—are available in the bulk food section in many grocery stores.
• The sauce will keep for up to a week in the fridge. To reheat, add a little water if it's thick, and then warm on the stove or in the microwave.

Pour the oil into a large wok or and set over medium heat until shimmering hot. Add the peanuts and stir and cook until golden brown, 4 to 6 minutes. Toss them continuously so they cook evenly without burning.

Scoop up the peanuts with a slotted spoon and transfer to a paper-towel lined plate to cool. Remove any burnt peanuts, they will taste bitter.

When the peanuts are cool enough to handle, grind them in a small food processor or pulverize them with a mortar and pestle until they have texture of coarse sand.

Mix the water together with the lime leaves, tamarind, sugar and salt in a medium saucepan. Bring to a boil over medium-high heat, then adjust the heat until it is bubbling gently. Simmer for about 5 minutes, breaking up the tamarind pulp.

Remove the lime leaves and any chunks of tamarind pulp with a slotted spoon. Add the ground peanuts and bring to a boil over medium-high heat. Adjust the heat and simmer gently until thick and creamy like gravy, 8 to 10 minutes, stirring often so the sauce doesn't stick to the bottom of the pot.

Remove from the heat and stir in the *sambal oelek* and Thai chilies (if using). Taste and adjust the seasonings as needed, making sure the acidity of the tamarind or lime sings through.

Serve the peanut sauce with vegetables or as a dipping sauce for grilled kebabs.

Sweet Chili Sauce

Traditionally, this sauce is thickened by boiling with lots of sugar. I add a plum instead, because its natural pectin helps thicken the sauce. Depending on your capsaicin tolerance, you can remove as many seeds from the chilies as you wish, or (if you veer toward the other end of the spectrum), add in a Thai chili or two. Keep in mind that the sauce will be quite spicy and tart at first, but the flavors will dissipate over time.

PREP TIME: 5 MINUTES
COOK TIME: 30 MINUTES
MAKES: 1½ CUPS (375 ML)

½ cup (90 g) chopped black or red plum (1 large plum)
5 cloves garlic, peeled
4 oz (115 g) fresh long red chilies like Fresno, stemmed, seeded as desired, and chopped
1 teaspoon fine sea salt
2 cups (500 ml) water
½ cup (125 ml) distilled white vinegar
4 thin slices fresh ginger
1 cup (200 g) granulated sugar, divided

Spicy Soy Dipping Sauce

Perfect with steamed or fried dumplings, this sauce is also made with Chinese black vinegar. A combination of soy sauce and rice vinegar makes a fine substitute.

PREP TIME: 5 MINUTES
MAKES: 1 CUP (250 ML)

½ cup (125 ml) soy sauce
⅓ cup (85 ml) rice vinegar
1 tablespoon toasted sesame oil
2 teaspoons *sambal oelek* (or to taste)
1 teaspoon granulated sugar
1 tablespoon slivered fresh ginger
1 tablespoon chopped green onions (scallions)
1 teaspoon toasted sesame seeds

Whisk together the soy sauce, vinegar, oil, *sambal oelek* and sugar in a medium bowl until the sugar completely dissolves. Garnish with ginger, green onions and sesame seeds. Set aside until ready to serve.

Place the chopped plum and garlic in a mini food processor and pulse until coarsely ground, about 15 seconds. Add the chilies and salt and continue pulsing until the mixture becomes a paste. Little bits of chili are fine. Set aside.

Combine the water, vinegar, and ginger in a large saucepan and set over medium-high heat. Stir in ¾ cup (150 g) of the sugar. When it has dissolved, add the chili mixture. Bring to a boil, then reduce the heat until it bubbles gently and simmer for 40 to 50 minutes, or until the liquid has thickened and reduced to 1½ cups. Stir occasionally to prevent it from sticking to the bottom.

Remove from the heat and allow to cool uncovered. Taste and add part or all of the remaining ¼ cup (50 g) more sugar as needed. Once the sauce has cooled completely, remove the ginger and transfer to a lidded jar. Keeps in the refrigerator for several months.

Easy Peanut Sauce

Peanut sauce must be the most popular Southeast Asian sauce making the rounds in U.S. restaurants. It goes with everything from grilled meats to tofu to vegetables, and this version is easy to make at home. You can also substitute coconut milk for up to half the water to make a thicker, richer sauce.

PREP TIME: 5 MINUTES
MAKES: 1 CUP

½ cup (125 ml) smooth unsweetened peanut butter
2 cloves garlic, peeled
2 tablespoons fresh lime juice (from 1 large lime)
1 teaspoon fine sea salt
1 tablespoon coconut palm sugar or 2 teaspoons dark brown sugar
1 fresh long red chili like Fresno, chopped and stemmed, seeded as desired, or 1 teaspoon *sambal oelek* (to taste)
1 to 2 Thai chilies (optional)
½ cup (125 ml) warm water

In a blender or food processor, blitz the peanut butter, garlic, lime juice, salt, sugar, chilies and water until the mixture is smooth. Transfer the sauce to a bowl and set aside. The sauce may be made up to 2 days in advance if kept covered and chilled.

> *Tip* If you don't have a blender or food processor, mix the peanut butter with hot water until a smooth paste is formed. Add the remaining ingredients (run the garlic through a press) and mix well.

Soy Sauce and Vinegar Pickled Radishes

Red-skinned radishes look striking against the dark-colored brine, and taste delicious too!

PREP TIME: 10 MINUTES
COOK TIME: 5 MINUTES
MAKES: 2 CUPS (500 ML)

1 bunch (about 12) red radishes, sliced

Pickling Brine
¼ cup (60 ml) Dashi Seaweed Stock (page 29)
¼ cup (60 ml) soy sauce
¼ cup (60 ml) rice vinegar
¼ cup (50 g) granulated sugar

Combine the dashi, soy sauce, vinegar and sugar in a small pot over medium heat and cook until the sugar melts, 4 to 5 minutes. Remove from the heat and allow the brine to cool.

Place the radishes in a pint (500 ml) glass jar and pour in the brine. Refrigerate overnight, stirring the radishes periodically to coat them evenly. Serve.

Homemade Spicy Kimchi (Fermented Chinese Cabbage)

Chinese or napa cabbage is the most common vegetable used to make Korean kimchi. But once you think out of the vegetable box, the possibilities are endless! Simply be inspired by what you find at the farmers' market or grocery store.

PREP TIME: 15 MINUTES + SALTING, DRYING
  AND FERMENTING TIME
MAKES: 1 QUART (1 LITER)

1 medium head Chinese cabbage (about
  2 lbs/1 kg)
2 tablespoons fine sea salt or kosher salt

Seasoning Paste

2 tablespoons minced garlic (about
  6 cloves)
Chubby ½-in (1.5-cm) knob fresh ginger,
  peeled and grated
1 teaspoon granulated sugar
2 to 3 tablespoons Dashi Seaweed Stock
  (page 29) or water
3 tablespoons Korean red pepper powder
  (or to taste)
4 green onions (scallions), white and green
  parts, cut into 1-in (2.5-cm) pieces
¼ cup (50 g) sliced yellow onion

Cut the cabbage lengthwise into quarters and remove the cores. Cut each quarter crosswise into 2-in (5-cm) wide strips.

Place the cabbage and salt in a large bowl and massage the salt into the cabbage using your hands. Let stand for 1 hour.

Rinse the cabbage under cold running water to remove all traces of salt and drain in a colander for 15 to 20 minutes.

While the cabbage is salting, make the Seasoning Paste. Stir together the garlic, ginger, sugar, and dashi or water in a large bowl (it should be large enough to hold the cabbage, too) to form a smooth paste. Mix in the red pepper powder.

Add the green onions and yellow onion to the seasoning paste and mix well. Press out any excess water from the cabbage and add it to the bowl. Gently work the paste into the vegetables with your hands until they are thoroughly coated. I recommend wearing plastic gloves to protect your hands.

Pack the kimchi tightly into a quart-sized (1 liter) glass jar (a wire bail works well), pressing down as you fill it, until the brine rises above the vegetables. Leave at least 1 inch (2.5 cm) at the top and seal with the lid.

Let the jar stand at room temperature for about 3 days. Place a plate underneath to catch any overflow as the kimchi ferments and expands. You may see bubbles inside the jar; this is just another sign the kimchi is fermenting. Taste daily, and when the kimchi tastes ripe enough for you, refrigerate. Consume within a year.

> *Tip* Use only nonreactive wooden utensils and glass/ceramic bowls for prep (no metal or plastic), and glass or ceramic jars for storage.

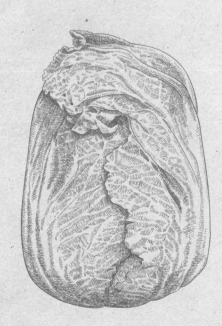

Quick Vinegar Daikon and Carrot Pickles

Many cultures use a similar pickling method. Daikon radish and carrots are a popular duo for Vietnamese noodle bowls and sandwiches.

PREP TIME: 15 MINUTES +
   30 MINUTES SALTING TIME
MAKES: 1 QUART

5 carrots (about 2 lbs/1 kg)
1 lb (500 g) daikon radish
2 teaspoons fine sea salt
1 cup (250 ml) hot water
1 cup (250 ml) rice vinegar
½ cup (100 g) granulated sugar
Dried red chilies, to taste (optional)
Ginger slices, to taste (optional)

Peel the carrots and cut crosswise into thirds. Slice each third lengthwise into three planks, and then cut each plank into matchsticks about ¼ inch (5 mm) thick. Cut the daikon radish to the same shape and size.

Place the carrots and daikon in a colander over the sink, sprinkle with the salt, and mix well. Let the vegetables sit for about 30 minutes to draw out moisture; this will allow the pickling brine to penetrate the vegetables more thoroughly for better texture and flavor. They should be soft and pliable after salting. Rinse briefly and drain the vegetables.

Make the brine while the vegetables are salting: combine the hot water, vinegar and sugar in a medium bowl and stir until the sugar dissolves completely.

Pack the carrots and daikon (and dried chilies or ginger, if using) into two 2-cup (500 ml) jars. Divide the brine between the two jars. Seal and refrigerate.

Steep for at least 2 hours and enjoy. The pickles will keep in the refrigerator for 4 weeks, if they're not gone by then!

Pickled Baby Bok Choy (Blanch First, Pickle Later)

I use this method to pickle greens like Chinese mustard cabbage. It's similar to the method used for Quick Vinegar Daikon and Carrot Pickles. The biggest difference is that the vegetable is blanched first so it keeps its color in the pickling brine.

TIME: 10 MINUTES
MAKES: 1 QUART

1 lb (500 g) baby bok choy
½ cup (125 ml) vinegar
½ cup (125 ml) water
½ cup (100 g) granulated sugar
1 tablespoon fine sea salt
Two ¼-in (5-mm) thick coins fresh ginger

Cut the bok choy leaves and stems into bite-sized pieces.

Fill a medium saucepan with water and bring to a boil. Add the bok choy and stir until the leaves darken, 2 to 3 minutes. Drain and plunge into ice water. Drain well, then pack into a 1-quart pickling jar.

Bring pickling sauce ingredients to a boil in a small pot, stirring to dissolve the sugar and salt. Pour over bok choy and add the ginger. Press down to remove any air bubbles. Refrigerate for 3 to 5 days before eating.

PICKLE TYPE	SPRING	SUMMER	AUTUMN	WINTER
Kimchi	Asparagus Red radishes	Corn Fennel	Brussels sprouts Savoy cabbage	Kale Pears
Soy sauce and vinegar pickles	Jalapeno peppers Ramps	Eggplant Zucchini	Beets Onions	Chinese cabbage Turnips
Quick vinegar pickles	French breakfast radishes Sugar snap peas	Cucumbers Mustard greens	Cauliflower Watermelon radish	Carrots Celery

How to Blanch Vegetables

Have ready a large bowl of ice water, a slotted spoon, and a plate lined with a kitchen towel or paper towel.

Bring a large pot of water to boil over high heat. Add a tablespoon or two of salt, if desired (it helps maintain color and adds flavor). If you are preparing a large quantity of vegetables, blanch in small batches to keep the water boiling. If you're blanching more than one type of vegetable, blanch each one separately.

Blanch pale vegetables like bean sprouts ahead of darker-colored ones like carrots to keep colors true.

When the color changes (usually between 2 and 5 minutes), use the slotted spoon to transfer the vegetables to the ice bath. (Also called "shocking," this stops the cooking process.) When the vegetables are completely cool, transfer them to the towel-lined plate to drain.

Broiled Tofu

Broiled tofu is an easy and tasty protein addition to many of the dishes in this book. Choose your marinade according to your preference and the accompanying dish.

PREP TIME: 5 MINUTES
COOK TIME: 6 MINUTES
MAKES: 4 SERVINGS

16 oz (500 g) firm or extra-firm tofu
Choice of marinade

Chinese-Style Hoisin Marinade

1 tablespoon hoisin sauce
1 tablespoon vegetable oil
1 tablespoon soy sauce

Japanese-Style Miso Marinade

1 tablespoon miso paste
2 teaspoons granulated sugar
1 teaspoon soy sauce
1 teaspoon mirin
2 teaspoons vegetable oil
½ teaspoon grated ginger
1 tablespoon green onions (scallions)

Indonesian-Style Soy Marinade

1 tablespoon soy sauce
1 tablespoon vegetable oil
1 teaspoon warm water
2 tablespoons coconut palm sugar or
  1½ tablespoons dark brown sugar

> **Tips** Broiled tofu can be made ahead and stored in the refrigerator for 3 to 4 days.
> • You can easily double this recipe and have broiled tofu on hand to add to your meals all week long.
> • If you prefer, you can cut the tofu into larger slabs, broil, then cut into batons.

Drain the tofu, or, if you're in a rush, pat it dry with paper towels. Cut into 8 squares or 16 triangles.

Whisk all marinade ingredients together in a shallow bowl.

Move the oven rack to the highest level. Preheat broiler on high (550°F/290°C).

Lightly grease a baking sheet. Coat each tofu piece with marinade on both sides. Lay tofu pieces on the sheet about 1 inch (2.5 cm) apart.

Broil the tofu pieces for about 3 minutes, until the tops brown. Turn over and broil for 2 to 3 more minutes until golden and crisp around the edges.

Baked Tofu

Baking tofu is a great alternative to frying. You'll still get a nice meaty texture, but without the grease.

PREP TIME: 5 MINUTES
COOK TIME: 40 MINUTES
MAKES: 2 SERVINGS

8 oz (250 g) extra-firm or firm tofu
2 teaspoons vegetable oil
½ teaspoon fine sea salt

Preheat oven to 350°F (175°C).

Drain the tofu (page 23) and cut into 1-inch (2.5- cm) cubes. Toss with the oil and salt in a medium bowl. Lightly coat a baking sheet with cooking spray. Arrange the tofu on the sheet in one layer. Bake for 35 to 40 minutes or until light golden, turning halfway through. Remove from the oven and set aside until ready to use.

> *Tip* Baked tofu will keep at room temperature for 2 to 3 hours until ready to use. It can be refrigerated for 1 to 2 days.

Fried Golden Tofu

Add fried tofu to pump up the protein in vegetable dishes. It's also great as a snack with Sweet Chili Sauce or Easy Peanut Sauce.

PREP TIME: 5 MINUTES + 30 MINUTES DRAINING TIME
COOK TIME: 15 TO 20 MINUTES
MAKES: 6 TO 8 SERVINGS

16 oz (500 g) firm or extra-firm tofu
Vegetable oil, for frying

Drain the tofu (page 23) and cut it into slabs about 1 inch (2.5 cm) thick. Then cut into 1-inch (2.5-cm) cubes (or whatever size your recipes calls for).

Pour enough oil into a wok or Dutch oven to reach a depth of 1½ to 2 inches (5 cm). Heat to 350°F (175°C) (use a thermometer or see page 14 for deep-frying tips). Add 10 to 12 pieces of tofu (depending on the size of your vessel) and fry for 3 to 5 minutes until golden and crispy. Don't let them go dry and hard. Remove with a slotted spoon and drain on paper towels. Bring oil back up to temperature before cooking the next batch. Repeat until all the tofu is fried.

> *Tip* Fried tofu can be made ahead and stored in a sealed container in the fridge for 2 to 3 days.

SPRING RECIPES

After a long, dreary winter, the sight of shoots pushing up from the soft soil is a joy to behold. My heart soars at the thought of making all my favorite recipes with spring's bounty: Baby Turnips and Mushrooms in Coconut Soup; Ponzu Butter Vegetables; and Fresh Artichoke Hearts, Green Beans and Bell Peppers in Thai Red Curry Sauce. But Mother Nature bamboozles me over and over.

Every year, at the first sign of warm(er) weather, I trade my sweater and jeans for a tank top and shorts and head out to the farmer's market dreaming of all the dishes I'll make that aren't casseroles or root-vegetable based. Alas, cheeky spring is fond of playing tricks on me. In-

Green Tea Rice Soup (page 61)

Ponzu Butter Vegetables (page 58)

stead of tables groaning under the weight of ramps, rhubarb and asparagus, I find the all-too-familiar bunches of collard greens and kale, not to mention piles of pumpkins (no offense, winter vegetables, I love you, too) as I shiver my way through the market.

Thankfully, the chilly days eventually pass. And then, lo and behold, spring is in full swing! I eagerly snap up my spring staples: pea shoots

STARTERS & SNACKS

Spicy Korean
Green Onion Salad

Baby Turnips and Mush-
rooms in Coconut Soup

Flaky Chinese Pancakes
with Chive Blossoms

Crispy Spring Rolls

Vegetable Soup
with Rhubarb

FAMILY-STYLE DISHES

Asparagus in
Coconut Cream Sauce

Fresh Artichoke Hearts,
Green Beans and Bell Peppers
in Thai Red Curry Sauce

Blanched Baby Spinach
with Sesame Sauce

Broccolini with
Seasoned Soy Sauce

Ponzu Butter Vegetables

Wokked Romaine Lettuce

ALL-IN-ONE MEALS

Green Tea Rice Soup

Vietnamese Noodle Salad Bowls

Spring Fried Rice with
Asparagus and Cilantro

Sesame Noodles

"Everyday" Pad Thai

(to be stir-fried with garlic) and asparagus (to be bathed in a delicate lemongrass-coconut sauce).

Over the years, I've been determined to try my hand at some new-to-me vegetables. I once avoided rhubarb, but now it's found a place in my Vegetable Soup with Rhubarb. I haven't looked back since. A few years ago I discovered that garlic scapes are oh-so-tasty pickled. Fiddlehead ferns, another peculiar vegetable, turned out to be delicious when stir-fried with salted black beans. And for the days when spring hesitates and the blustery winds blow in, I'll combine morels with an abundance of spring vegetables for a stick-to-your-ribs spring stew.

Vietnamese Noodle Salad Bowls (page 62)

Spicy Korean Green Onion Salad

This salad, made from green onions (scallions), is often served alongside Korean barbecued meats. I've added lettuce hearts to cut the zing so you can eat the salad on its own. If you're lucky enough to have a Korean grocery store in your vicinity, you'll probably find pre-shredded green onions in big bags. If not, shredding them is a great exercise in patience.

PREP TIME: 30 MINUTES + 1 HOUR FOR SOAKING

MAKES: 4 SERVINGS

8 large green onions (scallions)
1 small romaine lettuce heart

Spicy Dressing
1 teaspoon minced garlic
1 tablespoon granulated sugar
1 tablespoon toasted sesame seeds
2 teaspoons Korean red pepper powder
2 tablespoons soy sauce
1 tablespoon sesame oil
2 teaspoons rice vinegar

Slice the green onions lengthwise into very thin ribbons about ⅛ in (3 mm) wide—as thin as linguine if you can. You'll need about 3 cups. I've found that using a combo of kitchen scissors and my fingers is most effective. Rinse under cold running water to remove the slime. Soak the green onions in ice water for an hour or more to tame their bite and to make cute curls.

To make the Spicy Dressing, whisk together the garlic, sugar, sesame seeds, red pepper powder, soy sauce, sesame oil and rice vinegar in a small bowl. Taste and add more sugar or vinegar to balance the sweet-tart flavors as needed. Set aside.

Just before you're ready to serve, shred the lettuce into ½-inch (1-cm) ribbons (you'll need about 2 cups/100 g). Drain the green onions in a colander over the sink and dry both vegetables in a salad spinner or between paper towels to soak up excess water. Place the vegetables in a serving bowl.

When ready to serve, pour the dressing over the vegetables a little at a time (doing so at the last minute helps retain the vegetables' crunch) as you toss them. You can toss with your hands, the traditional way (but do wear food-handling gloves); or with tongs. Stop pouring when the vegetables are glistening but not drenched. Serve immediately.

Baby Turnips and Mushrooms in Coconut Soup

Turnips are at their finest in spring and early summer. Their crunchy texture and bittersweet flavor are delicious in this Thai coconut soup (*tom kha*) paired with fresh porcini or other seasonal mushrooms. If you can't find baby turnips, regular turnips or daikon radishes are fine too. Just peel them and cut into bite-sized pieces.

PREP TIME: 10 MINUTES
COOK TIME: 20 MINUTES
MAKES: 4 TO 6 SERVINGS

1 lb (500 g) baby turnips, stalks and leaves removed

One 14-oz (400-ml) can unsweetened coconut milk

3 cups (750 ml) low-sodium vegetable stock

2 plump stalks lemongrass, trimmed and bruised

One 1-in (2.5-cm) piece fresh galangal, cut into 4 thin slices (optional)

3 Asian (kaffir) lime leaves, torn in half (optional)

8 oz (250 g) fresh porcini or other seasonal mushrooms, sliced

6 to 8 red Thai chilies, crushed with the butt of a knife

½ teaspoon granulated sugar

¼ cup (60 ml) soy sauce

¼ cup (60 ml) fresh lime juice (from 2 large limes)

¼ cup (5 g) coriander leaves (cilantro)

Scrub the baby turnips and cut each one into 8 wedges.

In a medium pot, combine the coconut milk, vegetable stock, lemongrass, galangal and lime leaves (if using). Place over medium heat and bring to a simmer.

Add the turnips and adjust the heat as needed to maintain a steady simmer. Don't let the soup come to a rolling boil or the coconut milk will curdle. Cook the turnips for about 3 minutes, and then add the mushrooms. Continue simmering until the turnips are tender (I like them al dente) and the mushrooms are soft, 10 to 12 minutes more. Test a piece of each to see if they're cooked to your liking. Add the chilies, sugar, soy sauce and lime juice. Taste and adjust seasonings if necessary. Remove the herbs and ladle the soup into individual bowls. Place 1 crushed chili in each bowl and garnish with the cilantro leaves. Serve immediately.

> *Tip* Ginger is often used as a substitute for galangal. In my opinion, their flavors are totally different and I'd rather omit than swap them. But if you don't mind the difference, go ahead and make the substitution.

Flaky Chinese Pancakes with Chive Blossoms

Instead of the green onions usually used in these pancakes, I've added chives and purple chive blossoms for a burst of color and a delicate flavor reminiscent of garlic and onions. Chive blossoms resemble powder puffs, and are unwieldy to eat whole. Before using them in dishes, remove their central stems first and then pull apart the florets. If you grow chives in your garden, you will have an abundance of these darling little blossoms. If not, you can often find them at farmers' markets at springtime. Chive blossoms aren't compulsory, however; go ahead and experiment with chives only, or whatever alliums catch your eye at the market—ramps, leeks, spring onions...your choice!

PREP TIME: 20 MINUTES +
  30 MINUTES RESTING TIME
COOK TIME: 10 MINUTES
MAKES: 4 TO 6 SERVINGS (FOUR PANCAKES)

2 cups (250 g) all-purpose flour, plus extra for dusting
⅔ cup (175 ml) just-boiled water
1 teaspoon fine sea salt, plus more for sprinkling
1 to 2 tablespoons sesame oil
½ cup (50 g) chopped chives and chive blossoms
Vegetable oil, for frying
Dipping Sauce (recipe follows)

Place the flour in a large mixing bowl and make a well in the middle. Slowly pour in the water, stirring with a wooden spoon and scraping the sides as you go. The dough will look like cheese curds. When it is cool enough to handle, knead into a ball with your hands. If it is still dry, add more water a tablespoon at a time until it just comes together.

Turn the dough out onto a lightly floured work surface. Knead until it forms a smooth, soft ball and is no longer sticky, adding more flour as needed. Place the dough in a lightly oiled bowl, cover with a damp towel and let rest for 30 minutes at room temperature.

Lightly flour the work surface again and turn the dough out. Knead for another 2 minutes. Divide the dough into 4 equal pieces and roll each piece into a smooth ball.

With a rolling pin, roll out one ball into a disk roughly 7 inches (17.5 cm) in diameter. Sprinkle with ¼ teaspoon salt and roll again. Brush with a thin layer of sesame oil, then sprinkle 2 tablespoons of chives and chive blossoms evenly over the dough, leaving a ½-in (1-cm) border on the edge. Roll the disk up like a jelly roll, then coil into a tight snail-like spiral, tucking the end under.

Flatten the spiral gently with your palm and roll it out again, this time into a ¼-inch (5-mm) thick pancake about 6 inches (15 cm) in diameter. If the chives start to poke out of the dough, just tuck them back in. Set the finished pancake aside and repeat with the remaining dough. (Pancakes can be made ahead: Stack them between layers of parchment paper and refrigerate for a few hours before frying.)

Prepare a paper-towel-lined plate or set a rack over a baking sheet.

Heat 1 tablespoon vegetable oil in an medium nonstick or cast-iron skillet over medium heat until shimmering hot. Fry the pancakes one at a time until golden brown and crispy on the bottom, 2 to 3 minutes. Carefully flip with a spatula, swirl in 1 teaspoon oil and cook until the second side is golden brown, another 1 to 2 minutes. Transfer to the plate or rack to drain excess oil and cover to keep warm while you make the rest of the pancakes. Repeat with the remaining dough. (If using a cast-iron skillet, keep in mind that they retain heat very well, so adjust the heat and cooking time as necessary.)

Cut each pancake into 6 wedges, sprinkle with additional salt (optional), and serve immediately with Dipping Sauce.

Dipping Sauce

¼ cup (60 ml) soy sauce
¼ cup (60 ml) rice vinegar
2 teaspoons granulated sugar
½ teaspoon minced fresh ginger
1 tablespoon finely sliced green
   onions (scallions), green parts only

Combine all ingredients in a medium bowl and whisk together until the sugar has dissolved.

Tips When frying pancakes, jiggle the pan once in awhile. (Someone told me that this creates a flakier pancake—I'm not sure it works, but it doesn't hurt to try!)
• To freeze, stack rolled, uncooked pancakes between layers of parchment and wrap securely in plastic wrap or foil. Cook frozen pancakes for 4 or 5 minutes on each side. Reheat cooked pancakes in a 450°F (230°C) oven for 4 to 5 minutes.

Crispy Spring Rolls

Spring rolls or egg rolls, call them what you will, this lovely snack is a perennial favorite. I've given it a new twist with jicama, but you can use more cabbage, bean sprouts and/or bamboo shoots as well. I shred my vegetables by hand, but if you have a matchstick slicer or food processor, go ahead and use it (aim for ⅛-in/3-mm shreds). Don't use a box grater, though— the vegetable pieces come out too thin and release too much water.

The thin, eggless wheat wrappers available at Asian markets turn into shatteringly crisp spring roll shells. I prefer them to the egg roll/pasta wrappers (Nasoya is one brand) available at many mainstream grocery stores. Those are easier to find, but they're very thick, and tend to come out doughy on the inside and blotchy on the outside.

PREP TIME: 45 MINUTES + TIME FOR SALTING

COOK TIME: 15 MINUTES

MAKES: 8 SERVINGS

1¼ lbs (550 g) jicama, cut into 2-in (5-cm) matchsticks

1½ cups (350 g) shredded cabbage

3 carrots, cut into 2-in (5-cm) matchsticks

2 teaspoons fine sea salt, divided

Vegetable oil, for frying

1 tablespoon minced garlic

½ cup (60 g) minced shallot

2 green onions (scallions), white and green parts, chopped and kept separate

½ cup (115 g) chopped celery stalks and leaves, kept separate

½ teaspoon freshly ground black pepper

½ teaspoon granulated sugar

Eighteen 8 x 8-in (20 x 20-cm) or twenty-four 6 x 6-in (15 x 15-cm) spring roll wrappers (plus extras), defrosted if frozen

Sweet Chili Sauce (page 37), for serving

To make the filling, place the jicama, cabbage and carrots in a colander and toss with ½ teaspoon of the salt. Drain over the sink or a large bowl for 30 minutes to release liquids. (Skip this step if you're in a rush.)

Swirl the oil into a large wok or skillet and set over medium-high heat until shimmering hot. Add the garlic, shallots and white parts of the green onion; cook until aromatic, about 30 seconds. Add the jicama, cabbage, carrots and celery stalks, followed by 1½ teaspoons salt, pepper and sugar. Stir and cook for 8 to 10 minutes, until the vegetables are tender-crisp (you can cook them longer if you prefer softer vegetables) and most of the liquid has evaporated. Stir in the green parts of the green onion and the celery leaves. Taste and adjust seasonings as needed. Remove from heat.

Wait 5 to 10 minutes for the filling to cool a little (spread it out on a large plate to speed up the process), then drain in a colander, pressing down with a wooden spatula to remove as much liquid as possible. You'll have about 4 cups of filling. The filling can be made one day ahead and refrigerated.

To assemble the spring rolls, set up your work station: Place the filling in a bowl; stack the wrappers with the smooth side down (don't worry if you can't figure this out, the smooth side just fries up nicer) and cover with a damp cloth so they don't dry out; line a bak-

ing sheet with parchment paper; and fill a small bowl with water.

Carefully peel off one wrapper and place it smooth-side-down on a clean, dry surface. Turn it like a diamond with the bottom tip pointing toward you. Scoop up filling (2 heaping tablespoons for a 8 x 8-in wrapper and 1 heaping tablespoon for a 6 x 6-in wrapper), squeeze to expel extra liquid, and place on the lower third of the wrapper.

Fold the bottom corner over the filling and tuck tightly underneath. Fold the left and right side corners toward the middle of the wrapper so that it looks like an open envelope, and then roll tightly into a log. Dab water along the top edge and finish rolling—tightly!—to seal. Place rolls seam-side down on the tray 1 inch (2.5 cm) apart. Repeat until all the spring rolls are assembled.

To fry, pour enough oil into a small pot or Dutch oven to reach a depth of 2 inches (5 cm). Set over medium-high heat until the temperature reaches 350°F (180°C) (use a deep-fry thermometer or see page 14 for deep-frying tips). Line a plate with paper towels or set up a rack over a baking sheet to drain the spring rolls. When the oil is hot, slip a few spring rolls in gently and fry, turning often, for 1 to 2 minutes or until golden all over. Remove with a slotted spoon and drain. Bring the oil back up to 350°F (180°C) and continue frying the rest of the spring rolls in batches.

To bake, preheat oven to 425°F (220°C). Place a rack on a baking sheet and brush with vegetable oil. Lightly brush each roll with vegetable oil and place rolls on the rack 1 in (2.5 cm) apart. Bake until golden on top, 15 to 20 minutes. Then turn over and bake until golden and crisp, 10 to 12 more minutes.

Serve immediately with Sweet Chili Sauce.

Tips The steps and time taken may seem daunting but spring rolls can be made in stages: make the filling on one day, assemble on the second, and cook on the third.

• To prevent the spring rolls from breaking or getting soggy, wait until the filling is completely cool and drain it of as much liquid as possible before assembling.

• When looking for wrappers, choose the thinnest you can possibly find. Any size or shape will do, you'll just have to adjust the amount of filling and cook time.

• Reheat cooked spring rolls in a 325°F (160°C) oven for 5 to 6 minutes until heated through. Unfortunately, they won't get as crisp in the oven as when freshly fried.

• If you plan to freeze them, arrange on the baking tray 1 in (2.5 cm) apart and freeze until hard, about 1 hour. Transfer to zip-top bags and freeze for up to a month.

• When cooking from frozen, do not thaw first. Fry or bake for 1 to 2 extra minutes. Check that the filling is cooked and not frozen. If still cold or frozen, add more cooking time.

Vegetable Soup with Rhubarb

When I first moved to the U.S., rhubarb was a vegetable (or is it a fruit?) that I didn't get. But one spring, I had an epiphany while I was sipping on a dish called *canh chua* at a Vietnamese restaurant in Seattle. The piquant flavor of tamarind, the usual sour ingredient in this soup, surprised me. I thought to myself, tamarind is sour, rhubarb is sour (I'd just seen some rhubarb at the farmer's market). I put two and two together, and voila— sour rhubarb soup was born! The rhubarb imparts a tang that's a little more coy than tamarind, but you end up with a pretty soup tinged a delicate pink. Plus, the rhubarb develops a soft, spongy texture akin to *bac ha* (taro stem), the vegetable traditionally added to this cleansing Vietnamese-style soup. Other vegetables and ingredients you might include are green beans, bok choy, okra and tofu.

PREP TIME: 15 MINUTES

COOK TIME: 10 MINUTES

MAKES: 4 SERVINGS

1 tablespoon vegetable oil

2 teaspoons minced garlic

1 small yellow onion, chopped

2 medium stalks rhubarb, halved lengthwise and chopped on the diagonal into ½-in (1-cm) slices

6 cups (1.5 liters) low-sodium vegetable stock

2 large firm, ripe tomatoes, cut into wedges

1 cup (200 g) pineapple cubes

2 cups (150 g) spring greens such as dandelion leaves or bok choy, cut into 2-in (5-cm) pieces

1½ tablespoons granulated sugar

1 tablespoon Vegan "Fish" Sauce (page 35)

1 cup (100 g) bean sprouts

Garnishes

Chopped coriander leaves (cilantro)

Chopped green onion (scallion)

Lemon wedges (optional)

Swirl the oil into a large pot and set over medium heat. When shimmering hot, add the garlic and onion and fry until the onion turns translucent, 1 to 2 minutes.

Add the chopped rhubarb and cook, stirring, for 1 to 2 minutes, until the rhubarb pieces soften and turn a shade paler. Pour in the vegetable stock and bring to a boil.

Add the tomatoes, pineapple and spring greens. Cook for another 1 to 2 minutes, until the tomatoes soften and the greens are cooked to your liking.

Stir in the sugar and the Vegan "Fish" Sauce. Taste and adjust seasonings as desired. Turn off the heat and add the bean sprouts; they will cook in the residual heat but still be crunchy. Pour the soup into a large communal bowl to be placed on the table for sharing, or scoop into individual bowls. Sprinkle with the coriander leaves and green onions to taste. Serve with lemon wedges, if desired.

Tip Rhubarb leaves contain high levels of oxalic acid and are poisonous. Remove all traces of the leaves before using the stalks.

Asparagus in Coconut Cream Sauce

I've always loved fresh, in-season asparagus drizzled with olive oil and simply grilled or broiled. But this quickly assembled dish with a mélange of bright flavors comes in as a close second—it's perfect for a weeknight meal. For an extra-special treat, make it with purple asparagus.

PREP TIME: 15 MINUTES
COOK TIME: 10 MINUTES
MAKES: 4 SERVINGS

2 tablespoons vegetable oil

1 tablespoon minced garlic

1 tablespoon peeled and grated (preferably young) fresh ginger

1 plump stalk lemongrass, trimmed and cut on the diagonal into thin ovals, or ½ teaspoon lemon zest and ½ teaspoon lime zest

2 teaspoons chili paste such as *sambal oelek*, or chili flakes

1 cup (250 ml) unsweetened coconut milk

½ cup (125 ml) water

1 lb (500 g) asparagus (preferably skinny stalks), tough root ends snapped off, cut into 2-in (5-cm) pieces, tips and stems separated

1 teaspoon fine sea salt

½ teaspoon soy sauce

1 tablespoon lime juice

10 Thai or Italian basil leaves, torn

Swirl the oil into a large wok or skillet and set over medium-high heat. When shimmering hot, add the garlic, ginger and lemongrass and fry until aromatic, about 30 seconds.

Stir in the chili paste and cook until the chili turns dark red. Pour in the coconut milk and water and simmer for 1 minute. Add the asparagus stems and simmer for 2 minutes. Add the tips and simmer for another 2 to 4 minutes. Stir in the salt, soy sauce, lime juice and basil leaves. Simmer for 1 to 2 minutes more, until the asparagus is tender. Taste and adjust seasonings as needed. Serve with steamed white rice.

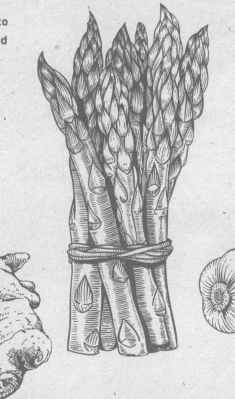

Fresh Artichoke Hearts, Green Beans and Bell Peppers in Thai Red Curry Sauce

Nothing compares to fresh artichokes in season. I usually steam them whole and munch on the leaves off the stem, saving the hearts for last. But the hearts are delicious in other dishes too. Removing them from a fresh artichoke is definitely fiddly work but the hearts are so sweet and tender, it's worth the extra effort. You can certainly buy precooked, water-packed (avoid the oil-packed ones) artichokes available in a jar or can. This will save you time. Feel free to use any vegetables you like in this dish. Snow peas, mushrooms, eggplant, etc. are all fair game.

PREP TIME: 20 MINUTES
COOK TIME: 10 MINUTES
MAKES: 4 SERVINGS

6 oz (170 g) fresh (see sidebar for prep) or store-bought precooked artichoke hearts

1 tablespoon vegetable oil

½ cup (75 g) sliced yellow onion

1 cup (250 ml) unsweetened coconut milk, divided

2 tablespoons store-bought red curry paste (I use Thai Kitchen brand)

¾ cup (190 ml) water

1 cup (175 g) sliced red bell pepper

6 oz (170 g) green beans, trimmed and snapped in half

2 medium carrots, peeled and sliced

3 Asian (kaffir) lime leaves (optional)

1 plump stalk lemongrass, trimmed and cut on the diagonal into thin ovals

½ teaspoon fine sea salt

2 tablespoons crushed roasted peanuts to garnish (optional)

If using store-bought artichoke hearts, rinse them first. Cut into bite-sized pieces.

Swirl the oil into a medium pot and set over medium heat until shimmering hot. Add the onion and cook until aromatic, about 30 seconds.

Add 3 tablespoons coconut milk and the red curry paste and stir until well combined. Add 2 more tablespoons coconut milk.

Raise the heat to medium-high and bring to a boil. Cook until the coconut oil separates from the mixture and rises to the surface; it will start to bubble, about 3 minutes. Stir in another 3 tablespoons of coconut milk and the water.

Add the bell pepper, green beans, carrots, fresh artichoke hearts (if using) and the rest of the coconut milk. Add more water to cover the vegetables if necessary. Raise the heat to high and bring to a boil again, then reduce heat to medium.

Crumple the lime leaves (if using) to release the essential oils and drop them into the pot. Add the lemongrass and stir. Adjust the heat until the curry is bubbling gently; simmer, partially covered, until the vegetables are tender-crisp, 6 to 7 minutes. If using precooked artichokes, add them now and cook for another 2 to 3 minutes, until the artichokes are heated through and the rest of the vegetables are cooked to your liking. Remove the pot from the heat and stir in the salt. Taste and add more salt as needed. Garnish with peanuts if desired and serve immediately with steamed jasmine rice.

Preparing Fresh Artichokes

If you can find baby artichokes, they're even easier to prep because you don't need to remove the fuzzy choke (the fibrous stuff in the middle).

PREP TIME: 15 MINUTES

2 large or 3 medium globe artichokes
  (2 lbs/1 kg total)
1 lemon, halved

Snap off the tough outer leaves by pulling them downward so they break off at the base. Stop when the leaves are pale green and tender.

Squeeze the juice from half a lemon into a medium bowl of water to cover the peeled artichoke hearts so they don't brown.

Trim the stem (don't cut it off—it's edible) and slice off the top third of the artichoke. With a paring knife, peel off the skin from the stem and smooth the rough areas around the base, removing any dark green sections. Squeeze lemon juice over exposed areas immediately after peeling. Cut the trimmed artichoke into quarters and remove the fuzzy choke in the middle with a spoon. Put finished pieces in the lemon water.

Steam the hearts for 8 to 10 minutes, or until tender.

Tip You can also steam the whole artichoke for 20 to 25 minutes. To eat, pull off the leaves, dip in vinaigrette and scrape a leaf against your teeth, pulling off the soft flesh. Save the hearts for the recipe.

Blanched Baby Spinach with Sesame Sauce

Kids and adults alike love this simple and tasty vegetable dish. Any seasonal leafy greens such as dandelion greens or fiddlehead ferns can be prepared this way. Even ho-hum broccoli and green beans get an upgrade when tossed with sesame sauce.

I like the addition of black sesame for color, but using all white seeds is fine too. For a protein-packed dish, add some firm tofu to the sesame seeds in the food processor.

PREP TIME: 15 MINUTES
MAKES: 4 SERVINGS

8 oz (225 g) baby spinach or spinach leaves
½ cup (75 g) shredded carrot
3 tablespoons toasted white sesame seeds
1 tablespoon toasted black sesame seeds
1 tablespoon soy sauce
1½ teaspoons sugar
2 teaspoons sesame oil

Tips This dish can be made ahead and refrigerated for up to 1 day.
• My recipe testers, Wing Fong and his family, were divided about the saltiness of this dish. Use low-sodium soy sauce or 2 teaspoons soy sauce and 1 teaspoon water if you prefer less salt.

Place the spinach and carrot in a heat-proof bowl. Pour in boiling water to cover the vegetables. Blanch for about 1 minute until the leaves turn dark green. Stir and drain in a colander over the sink. Rinse under cold running water, squeeze out excess water and wring into a ball. Set aside.

Pour the sesame seeds into a small food processor and process for 45 seconds to a minute, until the seeds resemble coarse cornmeal. Don't process for too long or it will turn into a sticky paste. Alternately, grind seeds with a mortar and pestle.

Combine the ground sesame seeds, soy sauce, sugar, and sesame oil in a serving bowl and mix to form a loose, coarse paste. Unravel the ball of vegetables and toss them with the sesame mixture until they are well coated (chopsticks are great for this task). Taste and adjust seasonings as needed.

Serve at room temperature or chilled.

Broccolini with Seasoned Soy Sauce

This is the go-to preparation for Chinese broccoli (*gailan*). Broccolini— a gailan-broccoli hybrid— has a similar flavor profile and goes just as well with this salty-sweet sauce. Broccoli or rapini would work just as well. If you prefer, steam or blanch the broccolini on the stovetop instead of using the microwave. Just please, please, please don't overcook it.

PREP TIME: 5 MINUTES

COOK TIME: 5 MINUTES

MAKES: 4 SERVINGS

One 12-oz (350-g) bunch broccolini, trimmed

2 tablespoons soy sauce

2 tablespoons Chinese cooking wine or dry sherry

1 teaspoon granulated sugar

1 teaspoon sesame oil

1 teaspoon flavored oil (garlic or shallot, pages 25–26) or vegetable oil

1 tablespoon Microwaved Crispy Garlic Bits (page 25)

1 tablespoon Fried Shallots (page 26)

Wash the broccolini and spread the stalks in a large shallow dish. It's okay if they're not in a single layer. Pour in about ¼ cup (60 ml) water and cover with a paper towel or microwave food cover (I love these!).

Microwave on high for 2 to 4 minutes until the vegetables turn bright green and are tender to the bite. I like the stems crisp, not soft and floppy. Microwaves vary in power, so after 2 minutes, keep microwaving in 30-second increments until the vegetables are cooked to your liking.

Combine the soy sauce, cooking wine, granulated sugar, sesame oil and shallot or garlic oil in a small bowl and whisk until the sugar dissolves. Microwave on medium for about 30 seconds if necessary. Drizzle the broccolini with the sauce and sprinkle with the Microwaved Crispy Garlic Bits and Fried Shallots. Cut the broccolini into thirds and serve with steamed jasmine rice.

Ponzu Butter Vegetables

Ponzu sauce (recipe follows) with butter may seem like an odd flavor combination, but it's quite popular in Japan, especially with mushrooms. Here, I've decided to mix and match different vegetables.

Choose a 1 to 1½ lbs (500 to 750 g) selection of in-season vegetables that you'll enjoy from tender-crisp to fully roasted, and cut them into similar shapes and sizes. Then you won't have to open the foil pouch to check on them.

PREP TIME: 20 MINUTES + 15 MINUTES
   MARINATING TIME
COOK TIME: 20 MINUTES
MAKES: 4 SERVINGS

¼ cup (60 ml) Homemade Ponzu
   Sauce (see opposite page)
½ teaspoon fine sea salt
½ teaspoon chili flakes (optional)
1 medium zucchini, cut into ¼-in
   (5-mm) thick rounds
4 oz (115 g) shiitake mushrooms,
   stemmed and halved
½ large red bell pepper, sliced
2 oz (60 g) green beans, trimmed
   and snapped in half
1 large carrot, sliced
½ medium yellow onion, sliced
4 to 5 thin lemon or lime slices
2 tablespoons unsalted butter

Combine the Homemade Ponzu Sauce, salt and chili flakes (if using) in a large bowl, and stir to combine. Add the vegetables to the sauce, toss to coat, and set aside for 15 minutes.

Set the rack just above the middle of the oven and preheat to 400°F (205°C).

Cut a 24-inch (60-cm) piece of heavy-duty aluminum foil, lay it on a baking sheet and fold it in half to mark the center. Mound the vegetables in the center of the left half of the foil. Drizzle with a tablespoon or two of excess sauce and arrange the lemon slices on top. Cut the butter into nuggets and dab randomly over the vegetables. Carefully fold the right half of the foil over the left and crimp all sides to seal, creating a neat pouch. Bake for 20 minutes, turning once.

Transfer the pouch to a plate. The vegetables will continue to cook in the pouch, so quickly cut it open with a sharp knife and carefully fold back the foil so steam can escape. Remove the lemon slices before serving. Serve directly from the pouch if desired.

Tip The vegetable pouch can also be grilled over medium heat in a closed grill for 20 minutes.

Homemade Ponzu Sauce

Ponzu— a tangy, citrus-based flavoring sauce popular in Japanese cuisine— is available ready-made at many Asian markets. However, like most sauces, homemade tastes best. Ponzu is traditionally flavored with yuzu, a citrus fruit, but because fresh yuzu is hard to find outside Japan, I've used lemon and orange juices instead. Bottled yuzu juice works fine, but Meyer lemons, if you can lay your hands on any, have a similar floral flavor and fragrance. That being said, any citrus you have on hand (limes, tangelos, grapefruit) will work.

PREP TIME: 10 MINUTES + STEEPING TIME
MAKES: ⅔ CUP (165 ML)

2 tablespoons mirin

Pinch of sugar (optional)

¼ cup (60 ml) soy sauce

2 tablespoons fresh lemon juice
  (preferably Meyer)

2 tablespoons fresh orange, lime,
  or grapefruit juice

2 tablespoons rice vinegar

¼ cup (60 ml) water

One 2-in (5-cm) square piece kombu
  or ¼ teaspoon kelp granules

Heat the mirin and sugar (if using) in a small saucepan over medium heat until it starts to bubble. Add the soy sauce and simmer over low heat for 5 minutes. Remove from heat and let cool. Pour into a glass jar with a tight-fitting lid and add the citrus juices, rice vinegar, water and kombu. Cover and refrigerate for 12 hours or overnight. (If you are rushed for time, let it steep for at least 2 hours.)

Strain the sauce through cheesecloth or a fine-mesh strainer into a container with a lid, gently squeezing or pressing out the liquid. Seal and refrigerate for up to 2 months.

> **Tips** Ponzu can be used as a chicken marinade, a dipping sauce for Sushi Hand Rolls (page 132) or *shabu-shabu* (Japanese hot pot), and as a salad dressing. You can also use it to make Japanese-style pickles.
> • If you don't have mirin, see page 20 for a substitute.

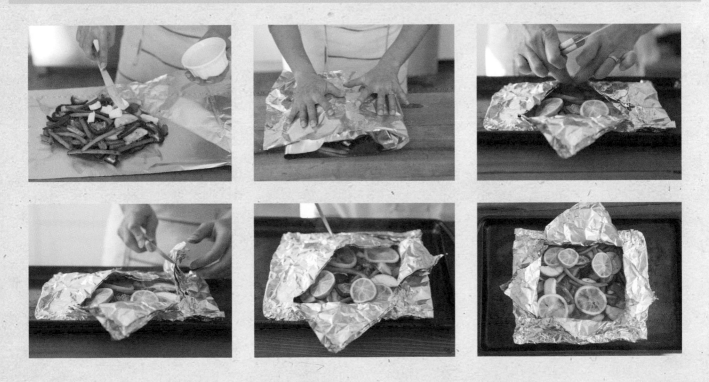

Wokked Romaine Lettuce

When my friend's mom first served me stir-fried iceberg lettuce with oyster sauce, I was skeptical. Not even oyster sauce can save iceberg lettuce, I thought. I was wrong! One day, tired of cold salads, I decided to stir-fry another common grocery store lettuce: romaine. Surprise, surprise! A brief toss in the wok transforms the lettuce. Its texture is softened by heat, and its flavor is sweetened by the sauce, which clings to every nook and cranny. Once you've mastered this basic dish, you can go wild— add ginger or slivered pork, and experiment with other stir-fry sauces.

PREP TIME: 5 MINUTES
COOK TIME: 5 MINUTES
MAKES: 4 SERVINGS

2 romaine lettuce hearts
1 tablespoon vegetable oil
1 tablespoon minced garlic
1 tablespoon soy sauce
½ teaspoon granulated sugar
1 teaspoon sesame oil
½ teaspoon toasted sesame seeds, for sprinkling

Trim the lettuce and cut crosswise into 1-inch (2.5-cm) wide pieces.

Preheat a wok or medium skillet over high heat for 1 minute. Swirl in the oil. When shimmering hot, add the garlic, then toss in the romaine lettuce in batches. Stir after adding each batch and wait until it cooks down a little before tossing more in. Stir and cook for 1 to 2 minutes, until the lettuce just starts to wilt.

Add the soy sauce and sugar. Cook, stirring, for about 1 minute more, until the lettuce is tender-crisp but still bright green. Drizzle the sesame oil over the lettuce and take off the heat. Sprinkle with sesame seeds and serve with steamed jasmine rice.

Green Tea Rice Soup

The Japanese name for this dish, *ochazuke*, means "tea and pickles"—referring to the key ingredients: Japanese green tea (not matcha, though) and pickles. Beyond that, anything goes. The pickles are a free-for-all: radishes, cucumbers, carrots... take your pick! Salmon is a popular traditional topping. For this vegan version, add any cooked (grilled, steamed, roasted) vegetables like carrots, green beans or squash. The typical Japanese garnishes—trefoil or shiso—are a little tough to find, so I use mint or watercress.

PREP TIME: 15 MINUTES
MAKES: 4 SERVINGS

4 cups (600 g) warm cooked white or brown
  Japanese sushi rice (leftover rice works fine)
8 teaspoons loose-leaf Japanese green tea like
  genmaicha, sencha, or hojicha
4 cups (1 liter) filtered or spring water
1 green onion (scallion), green and white parts,
  chopped
2 tablespoons toasted sesame seeds
Wasabi paste, to taste (optional)
Soy sauce, to taste (optional)

Tips If you want to make it more of a meal, you can add scrambled eggs seasoned with a splash of soy sauce and mirin.
 • This dish can be made with Dashi Seaweed Stock (page 29) instead of tea.
 • For a cool summertime treat, serve Green Tea Rice Soup with cold rice and cold tea.

Rice Toppings

½ cup (30 g) crushed savory Japanese rice crackers
½ cup (5 g) shredded or crumbled nori or Kale "Chips" (page 26)
½ cup (50 g) Soy Sauce and Vinegar Pickled Radishes (page 38) or cucumber pickles
½ cup (15 g) baby arugula (rocket) or mizuna leaves
1 cup (150 g) cooked, sliced carrots or other vegetables
Handful of mint or watercress leaves, torn or chopped

Divide the cooked rice among 4 large bowls. Have diners create their own flavors by adding toppings and seasonings to their liking.

Brew the tea by placing the tea leaves in a strainer in a large teapot. Heat the water in a kettle until it comes just short of boiling, about 185°F (85°C) for genmaicha. Steep the tea for 1 to 2 minutes. The exact amount of time will depend on the particular tea and personal preference. You may have to make several batches of tea depending on the size of your teapot. The ratio of tea leaves to hot water should be 2 teaspoons tea to 1 cup (250 ml) water.

Pour enough hot tea into each bowl to reach halfway up the rice. Allow the rice and tea to sit for about a minute to allow the flavors to meld.

Garnish with green onions and sesame seeds. Stir in a small dollop (about ⅛ teaspoon) of wasabi and/or a splash (about ¼ teaspoon) of soy sauce, if desired. Eat immediately.

Vietnamese Noodle Salad Bowls

Cool and refreshing, Vietnamese noodle salads are a lively contrast of tastes, textures and temperatures. The noodles sit on a bed of herbs and vegetables at room temperature, and are topped with warm shiitake mushrooms and tofu. This dish has many components to it, but you can prepare the noodles, greens and garnishes in advance. Just cover with damp towels and refrigerate. At serving time, assembly takes mere minutes.

PREP TIME: 30 MINUTES
COOK TIME: 25 MINUTES + 30 MINUTES SITTING TIME
MAKES: 4 SERVINGS

8 oz (225 g) dried round rice noodles (*bùn*, page 17)

Dipping Sauce
¼ cup (50 g) granulated sugar
¾ cup (175 ml) warm water
¼ cup (60 ml) fresh lime juice (from 2 large limes)
¼ cup (60 ml) Vegan "Fish" Sauce (page 35)
1 teaspoon chili paste like *sambal oelek* (optional)
1 clove garlic, minced

Vegetable Bed
2 cups (180 g) shredded lettuce (romaine, butter, red or green leaf)
2 cups (200 g) bean sprouts
1 cup (25 g) assorted herbs plucked off their stems (mint, Thai or Italian basil, cilantro)
1 large cucumber, cut into matchsticks

Toppings
8 Broiled Shiitake Mushrooms, sliced (page 64)
8 pieces Broiled Tofu (page 42)

Garnish
½ cup (75 g) Quick Vinegar Daikon and Carrot Pickles (page 40)
¼ cup (30 g) crushed roasted peanuts

Tip Extra Dipping Sauce can be used for Crispy Spring Rolls (page 50) or tossed with greens.

To cook the rice noodles, bring a large pot of water to a rolling boil over high heat. Add the noodles and cook until the strands are chewy-soft, 3 to 5 minutes. Rinse with cold running water until the noodles are cool and the water runs clear. Drain in a colander over the sink for 30 minutes. Set aside for up to 2 hours at room temperature. If saving for longer, cover and refrigerate for up to 1 day.

To make the Dipping Sauce, stir together the sugar, water, lime juice, Vegan "Fish" Sauce, chili paste (if using) and garlic in a medium bowl. Taste and adjust the seasonings as needed. You'll get about 1½ cups. This can be made up to 2 days ahead and refrigerated.

If you have refrigerated any of the components, take them out of the refrigerator 30 minutes before you are ready to serve.

When you are ready to serve, divide the lettuce, bean sprouts, herbs, and cucumber among 4 large soup or pasta bowls. Fluff the noodles and nest them on top of the vegetables. Arrange 2 mushroom caps and 2 tofu pieces (the toppings should be warm) on top of the noodles. Pour about ¼ to 1/3 cup (60 to 80 ml) of Dipping Sauce into 4 small bowls (one for each diner).

Serve the noodle bowls accompanied by the small bowls of Dipping Sauce and garnishes on plates for diners to pick and choose. To eat, pour the sauce over the noodle salad and toss a few times with chopsticks. Or, pick up individual bites with chopsticks and dip them in the sauce as you go.

Spring Fried Rice with Asparagus and Cilantro

Come springtime, recipes for spring risotto flood my consciousness and my inbox. Just about every food magazine and food website offers a riff on this classic Italian rice dish with the season's first asparagus or morels. "But why not spring fried rice?" I asked myself. Hence, this dish was born. I prefer asparagus of small to medium girth for this dish; save the fat ones for the oven or grill. Top each serving with a fried egg for some protein, if you'd like.

PREP TIME: 15 MINUTES
COOK TIME: 15 MINUTES
MAKES: 4 SERVINGS

3 tablespoons vegetable oil
2 cloves garlic, minced
1 large shallot or ½ small red onion, thinly sliced
2 fresh long red chilies like Fresno, stemmed, seeded as desired, and sliced, or 2 teaspoons chili paste (optional)
12 oz (340 g) asparagus, cut on the diagonal into 1-in (2.5-cm) pieces, tender tips and stems separated

4 cups (600 g) cold, cooked white rice (preferably jasmine or other long-grain rice)
2 tablespoons soy sauce
1/8 teaspoon fine sea salt
1/8 teaspoon freshly ground black pepper
Pinch of granulated sugar
2 green onions (scallions), green and white parts, chopped into 1-in (2.5-cm) lengths
¼ cup (15 g) fresh coriander leaves (cilantro), chopped, plus more for garnish

Swirl the oil into a large wok or skillet and set over high heat. When shimmering hot, add the garlic and shallots and fry until aromatic, about 30 seconds. Add the chilies and asparagus stems and cook until the asparagus turns bright green, about 1 minute. Add the tips and stir and cook for 1 or 2 more minutes.

With wet hands, break up the large clumps of rice. Add the rice to the wok. Stir and cook, breaking up any remaining clumps with a spatula, until the rice is heated through, 2 to 3 minutes. Add the soy sauce, salt, pepper and sugar, and toss to coat the rice and asparagus thoroughly. Taste and adjust seasonings as needed.

Add the green onions and coriander leaves. Continue to cook, stirring, until the green onions wilt, 15 to 30 seconds.

Divide among 4 plates, garnish with more coriander leaves, and serve immediately.

Broiled Shiitake Mushrooms

You can broil the mushrooms and tofu for the Vietnamese Noodle Salad Bowls (page 62) at the same time. The mushrooms may have to come out a little sooner. If you can't find shiitakes, 2 or 3 portobello mushroom caps (depending on size) will do the trick.

PREP TIME: 5 MINUTES + 1 HOUR MARINATING TIME
COOK TIME: 5 MINUTES
MAKES: 4 SERVINGS

1 small garlic clove, minced
1½ teaspoons minced shallot
1 Thai chili, chopped
2 teaspoons granulated sugar
¼ teaspoon freshly ground black pepper
2 tablespoons fresh lime juice
2 tablespoons soy sauce
2 tablespoons vegetable oil
8 small shiitake mushrooms, stems removed

Combine the garlic, shallot, chili, sugar, black pepper, lime juice, soy sauce and oil in a bowl big enough to hold the mushrooms. Mix until the sugar dissolves. Add the mushrooms and marinate for 1 hour.

Move the oven rack to the topmost rung. Preheat the broiler on high (550°F/290°C).

Line a baking sheet large enough to hold the shiitakes in a single layer with foil. Drain the mushrooms, reserving the marinade, and arrange at least 1 in (2.5 cm) apart on a baking sheet. Broil for 2 minutes. Flip and baste with the marinade. Broil for 1 to 2 minutes more, until the caps are soft, deep brown and shiny, and a little crisp on the edges. Cool and slice. The mushrooms will keep in the fridge for 2 to 3 days. Warm them up before serving.

Sesame Noodles

The biggest difference between Chinese sesame paste and tahini, its Middle Eastern counterpart, is that Chinese sesame paste is made of toasted white sesame seeds, and commercial tahini is typically made from raw hulled seeds. But you could use tahini in a pinch; just add a little toasted sesame oil to adjust the flavor.

The mild-tasting baby radishes like French Breakfast and other heirloom varieties that start appearing in spring make a fun and tasty topping for this simple cold dish. But use whatever radish you can find.

PREP TIME: 20 MINUTES
COOK TIME: 5 MINUTES
MAKES: 4 SERVINGS

1 lb (500 g) fresh Chinese egg noodles, or 8 oz (225 g) dried spaghetti

3 tablespoons sesame oil, divided

3 tablespoons soy sauce

2 tablespoons rice vinegar

3 tablespoons Chinese sesame paste

2 tablespoons smooth peanut butter

1 tablespoon honey or maple syrup

1 tablespoon grated fresh ginger

1 tablespoon minced garlic

2 teaspoons chili paste like *sambal oelek*

2 to 3 tablespoons warm water

2 mini seedless cucumbers, such as Persian, peeled and cut into matchsticks

½ cup (75 g) carrot matchsticks

½ cup (30 g) French Breakfast or other red radishes, trimmed and thinly sliced

2 green onions (scallions), green parts only

¼ cup (30 g) crushed roasted peanuts

Bring a large pot of water to a boil. Cook the noodles according to package directions until al dente. Drain, rinse with cold water, drain again and toss with 1 tablespoon of the sesame oil.

Whisk together the remaining 2 tablespoons sesame oil, soy sauce, vinegar, sesame paste, peanut butter, honey, ginger, garlic, and chili paste in a medium bowl. Add water, 1 table-spoon at a time, until the sauce reaches the consistency you like. I like mine as thick as heavy cream.

Pour ¾ of the sauce over the noodles, toss and taste. Add more or stop there. Transfer to a serving bowl and garnish with the cucumber, carrot, radishes, green onions and peanuts.

Tip If you have an abundance of toasted sesame seeds in your pantry, you can make your own sesame paste. (To toast, see page 25.) Pour 1 cup (150 g) toasted sesame seeds into your food processor and process for 2 to 3 minutes until a crumbly paste forms. Add 3 tablespoons of vegetable oil and process for another 1 to 2 minutes, scraping down the sides as necessary, until the paste reaches the desired consistency. To make a thinner paste, add 1 to 2 more tablespoons of oil. Makes ¾ to 1 cup (250 to 350 g), depending on how much oil you use). Transfer to a jar. Will keep in the fridge for 2 to 3 months.

"Everyday" Pad Thai

Pad Thai is commonly served with shrimp and chicken. But if you're going vegetarian, any seasonal vegetable is a contender. In spring, that means sugar snap peas, pea shoots, asparagus and more. I decided to go with the broccoli and carrots for this recipe, though. When it comes to finding the right noodle, pick a medium-width rice noodle about the size of linguine (if in doubt, wider is better — overly skinny noodles will break up when you stir-fry). However, the noodles will taste good no matter how wide they are.

PREP TIME: 20 MINUTES
COOK TIME: 10 MINUTES
MAKES: 2 SERVINGS

2 tablespoons and 1 teaspoon vegetable oil, divided
1 cup (100 g) broccoli florets
1 medium carrot, peeled and sliced on the diagonal
1 teaspoon Vegan "Fish" Sauce (page 35)
4 oz (125 g) Fried Golden Tofu (page 43), cut into 1 x ½ x ¼-in (2.5 x 1 x 0.5-cm) rectangles
2 cloves garlic, chopped
1 large shallot or ½ small red onion, sliced
2 tablespoons preserved radish (preferably sweet), soaked for 5 minutes, squeezed dry and chopped
6 oz (175 g) ¼-in (5-mm) wide dried rice noodles, soaked in warm water for 15 minutes and drained
2 large eggs, lightly beaten
½ cup (125 ml) Tamarind Sweet and Sour Sauce (recipe follows)
4 green onions (scallions) chopped into 2-in (5-cm) lengths
1½ cups (150 g) bean sprouts

Garnishes
Crushed roasted peanuts
Roasted chili flakes
1 lime, cut into wedges

Tips Pad Thai, like any stir-fried noodle dish, should be made in small batches. If you've seen Thai street vendors at work, you know that they usually make one serving at a time. If cooking for a crowd, I'd still advise you to make at most two servings at a time.

• Sweet preserved radish is an important component for making traditional pad Thai. However, finding any type of preserved radish whatsoever can be challenging. So be happy with whatever you may find. But please don't fret if you can't find it at all.

Swirl 1 tablespoon of the oil into a large wok or skillet and set over high heat until shimmering hot. Add the broccoli and carrots, sprinkle the Vegan "Fish" Sauce over, and stir and cook for 2 minutes. Add 2 tablespoons water and cover. Cook the vegetables until they're tender-crisp and the broccoli turns bright green, 1 to 2 minutes more. Set aside.

Wipe out the wok, then swirl in 1 tablespoon of oil and set over medium-high heat. Add the tofu and toss in the wok for a few seconds, followed by the garlic, shallot, and preserved radish, stirring between each addition. Stir and cook for 1 more minute. Add the noodles and stir and cook until soft, about 2 minutes. Push all the ingredients to one side. Add the remaining 1 teaspoon oil to the clear space and break in the eggs. Let the eggs cook undisturbed until the bottom just sets, 1 to 2 minutes. Then use a spatula to break it up into large curds and toss with the rest of the ingredients.

Add the Tamarind Sweet and Sour Sauce and mix well to coat the noodles evenly. Taste and adjust the seasonings as needed: Add more Tamarind Sweet and Sour Sauce for tamarind flavor, more Vegan "Fish" Sauce to make it saltier, or sugar for extra sweetness. If the noodles are not tender, add water, 1 tablespoon at a time, to soften them up.

Stir in the green onions and bean sprouts. Once they are mixed into the noodles and heated through, turn off the heat. Divide between 2 dinner plates. Serve immediately, accompanied by garnishes in small dishes alongside.

Tamarind Sweet and Sour Sauce

I was so excited when I first saw granulated coconut palm sugar at the supermarket. I've always had to shave off paper-thin slices from a hard block of palm sugar. If you can't find it, or just don't want to buy a half-pound bag, use brown sugar— you'll want to cut down on the amount, though, as it is sweeter.

PREP TIME: 45 MINUTES
MAKES: ABOUT 4 CUPS (1 LITER)

8 oz (250 g) wet tamarind (about ¾ cup)
3 cups (375 ml) water, divided
1½ cups (300 g) coconut palm sugar or 1¼ cups (225 g) dark brown sugar
⅓ cup (85 ml) Vegan "Fish" Sauce (page 35)

Combine the tamarind and 2 cups of the water in a medium pot. Heat over medium heat for 8 to 10 minutes, stirring, separating, and smashing with a wooden spoon until the tamarind turns into a thick and mushy mixture like peach purée.

Taking a spoonful at a time, push the mixture through a fine-mesh sieve to yield about 1½ cups (375 ml) of pulp.

Combine the leftover seeds, skin, and fiber with 1 cup warm water and stir to release more pulp. Push through the sieve again to yield 1 cup (250 ml) of runnier pulp. You will have 2½ cups (625 ml) of tamarind pulp in all.

Return the pulp to the pot. Stir in the coconut palm sugar and Vegan Vegan "Fish" Sauce. Bring to a gentle boil over medium heat and simmer for about 10 minutes, stirring to dissolve the sugar. Taste and add more seasonings to balance the sweet-salty-sour flavors to your liking.

Cool and pour into jar (it doesn't have to be fancy! I use a spaghetti jar). This sauce can be used for pad Thai, to stir-fry shrimp or to marinate chicken. It will keep in the refrigerator for up to a month.

SUMMER RECIPES

I love summer! Not just for the warm, sunny weather reminiscent of my childhood home but also for the glorious produce that becomes available when the temperature surges above 65°F or 18°C.

I've always been taught that a delicious meal starts with good ingredients. Think about in-season vegetables: they're so full of natural flavor you hardly have to do anything with them. And summer is the best season to realize this. Just tug a sugar snap pea off the vine and pop it into your mouth— you'll understand.

Although many grocery stores hasten summer by importing lackluster produce before its time, patience has its rewards. When the time does come, I head to the farmers' market eager to greet my favorite vegetables amidst a delirium of scent and color. I find voluptuous ruby-red tomatoes, shiny

Stir-Fried Heirloom Tomatoes and Egg (page 80)

Spicy Fried Okra (page 83)

purple eggplant, and the sweetest, freshest corn, and caress them as if they were long-lost friends. Importantly, I can make my purchases in full confidence knowing that the vegetables are at their peak quality, and undeniably sweet and flavorful.

I'm spoiled for choice when it comes to summer produce. Herbs— strongest in summer— find their way into Summer Herb

STARTERS & SNACKS

Fresh Salad with Sweet, Sour, Spicy Sauce

Golden Fresh Corn Fritters

Hand-Tossed Cabbage and Tomato Salad

Edamame with Chili Salt

Egg Flower Soup with English Peas and Sweet Corn

FAMILY-STYLE DISHES

Grilled Vegetable Kebabs with Two Marinades

Thai Basil Zucchini

Turmeric Zucchini and Carrot Stir-Fry

Stir-Fried Heirloom Tomatoes and Egg

Mixed Vegetable Salad with Indonesian Peanut Sauce

Eggplant with Red Pepper-Tomato Sauce

Spicy Fried Okra

ALL-IN-ONE MEALS

Eggplant "Meatball" Banh Mi Vietnamese Sandwich

Cambodian Sweet Soy Noodles with Pickles

Summer Herb Rice Salad

Buckwheat Noodles and Shoyu Dipping Sauce

Crispy Noodles with Savory Vegetables

Rice Salad. Lettuces are tossed into kaleidoscopic salads bumped up heartily with protein, and raw zucchini is transformed into a Korean-style side dish with sesame oil and lemon juice.

While salad-tossing and grilling are de rigueur, summer is also a fabulous time to stir-fry! It sounds counterintuitive, I know. Who wants to stand in front of a hot stove in the heat of summer? Thankfully, stir-frying is a quick and efficient cooking method.

Inevitably, I conjure up some of my favorite stir-fries — Stir-Fried Heirloom Tomatoes and Egg, Spicy Fried Okra, Thai Basil Zucchini and an ever-evolving "Whatever's Fresh at the Market" stir-fry.

Skewering zucchini for Grilled Vegetable Kebabs with Two Marinades (page 76)

Fresh Salad with Sweet, Sour, Spicy Sauce

There are two ways to eat this refreshing Indonesian snack: Toss the cut fruit and vegetables with the dressing and serve family-style; or—my favorite way—dip pieces of fruit or vegetables into the flavorful dressing like you'd dip sliced apples into caramel sauce. The form of the pieces doesn't really matter, just as long as they're easy to pick up with fingers or toothpicks. Feel free to slice up any firm, tart and/or bland vegetable or fruit in season—honeydew melon, under-ripe peaches, Anjou pears, etc. The sauce is enough for about 5 to 6 cups (1 kg) of fruit and veggies.

PREP TIME: 30 MINUTES
MAKES: 4 TO 6 SERVINGS

1½ cups (250 g) ripe pineapple cubes
1 cup (120 g) jicama, cut into 1-in (2.5-cm) cubes
½ cup (30 g) quartered red radishes
1 mini seedless cucumber like Persian, cut into short spears
1 firm, tart apple like Granny Smith, cut into 12 slices and soaked in salted water to prevent browning
1 firm, underripe mango, cut into 1-in (2.5-cm) pieces

Sweet, Sour, Spicy Sauce

¼ cup (35 g) roasted peanuts
½ cup (90 g) coconut palm sugar or ⅓ cup (70 g) dark brown sugar
6 tablespoons prepared tamarind juice (page 67) or 4 tablespoons freshly squeezed lime juice
1 long, fresh red chili like Fresno, stemmed, seeded as desired, and sliced; or 1 to 2 teaspoons *sambal oelek*
½ teaspoon fine sea salt

Tip Instead of tamarind juice, you can use lime juice. I recommend reducing by 1 or 2 tablespoons (replace with water), but you should adjust the amount to suit your taste.

Arrange the vegetables and fruit on a large platter or in a bowl.

To make the Sweet, Sour, Spicy Sauce, blitz the peanuts in a small food processor until coarsely chopped, about 10 seconds. Reserve 1 tablespoon for garnish, then add the sugar, tamarind juice, chili and salt. Process until it is the consistency of caramel sauce. The sauce is supposed to be grainy, so don't over-process. Add water 1 teaspoon at a time if the sauce is too thick. Taste and add more salt or tamarind juice as needed (especially if substituting brown sugar and lime juice).

Spoon the sauce into a pretty bowl, garnish with the reserved peanuts, and serve with the cut vegetables and fruit on a platter. Alternately, toss sauce with fruit and vegetables and serve in a bowl.

Golden Fresh Corn Fritters

Tasting of sunshine and butter, corn kernels scraped right off the cob find their way into one of my favorite childhood snacks every summer. As a little girl, I'd sneak a fritter fresh from the wok while my mom was still frying them up. Since I never heeded her warnings, I almost always burnt my tongue! But biting into a hot, crisp-on-the-outside, pillowy-on-the-inside fritter flecked with super-sweet corn was totally worth it.

PREP TIME: 10 MINUTES
COOK TIME: 20 MINUTES
MAKES: 14 TO 16 FRITTERS

2 large ears fresh sweet corn, or 1½ cups
  (225 g) frozen sweet corn
1 clove garlic, minced
1 green onion (scallion), green and white
  parts, finely chopped
1 Asian (kaffir) lime leaf, very thinly
  shredded (optional)
6 tablespoons all-purpose flour
1 large egg
¼ cup (60 ml) water
½ teaspoon fine sea salt, plus more for
  sprinkling
⅛ teaspoon ground white or black pepper
⅛ teaspoon ground coriander powder
Vegetable oil, for frying

Tips Buy several ears of corn to make both this recipe and Egg Flower Soup with English Peas and Sweet Corn (page 74) later in the week. Scrape the corn kernels into a container with a tight-fitting lid as soon as you get home from the market. Refrigerate for 3 to 4 days, or freeze for up to a month.

Scrape the corn kernels from the cob (see page 74 for methods). You'll get about 1½ cups (300 g). Combine the corn with the remaining ingredients, except the oil, in a medium mixing bowl, and stir to make a smooth batter.

Pour enough oil into a wok or large skillet to reach a depth of 1 inch (2.5 cm) and set over medium heat until shimmering hot.

Frying in batches, drop the batter gently into the hot oil by the heaping tablespoon. The patties will not be totally submerged. Spoon oil gently over the top of the fritters and cook until golden ruffles form around the edges, 2 to 3 minutes. Flip with a spatula and cook for another minute, until golden brown all over and cooked through.

Remove with a slotted spoon and drain on paper towels or a rack set over a baking sheet. Repeat until all the fritters are fried. Sprinkle with more salt as needed and serve immediately.

Hand-Tossed Cabbage and Tomato Salad

Several years ago, my friend Manda Mangrai's mom, Alvina, made a Burmese salad to pair with her flavorful curries when I visited. Alvina's salad lingered in my taste memory, and I came up with my own version using miso instead of dried shrimp for a punch of umami. A cornucopia of flavors and textures, this salad has more flair than coleslaw and will make a delightful change for your next barbecue. You can also use green tomatoes.

PREP TIME: 10 MINUTES
MAKES: 4 SERVINGS

2 tablespoons lime juice

1 teaspoon garlic oil (left over from frying garlic, page 25)

1 teaspoon Vegan "Fish" Sauce (page 35) or soy sauce

1 teaspoon white miso

1 teaspoon sesame oil

1 cup (100 g) finely shredded cabbage

3 medium tomatoes, cut into wedges

¼ cup (30 g) sweet onion, cut into thin crescents, soaked in water for 30 minutes to tame its bite

1 tablespoon Microwaved Crispy Garlic Bits (page 25), plus more for garnish

1 tablespoon Fried Shallots (page 26), plus more for garnish

2 tablespoons crushed roasted peanuts, plus more for garnish

1 tablespoon chopped coriander leaves (cilantro), for garnish

Whisk together the lime juice, garlic oil, Vegan "Fish" Sauce, miso and sesame oil vigorously in a large salad bowl. Add the cabbage, tomatoes and onion. Toss gently, preferably with your hands, but tongs or chopsticks work, too. Taste and adjust seasonings as needed. Sprinkle with the Microwaved Crispy Garlic Bits, Fried Shallots and peanuts; toss again with or without abandon. Garnish with more Microwaved Crispy Garlic Bits, Fried Shallots, peanuts and coriander leaves.

> *Tips* For convenience, you can buy a package of pre-shredded coleslaw cabbage from the grocery store
> • You may also replace the garlic oil with vegetable oil or more sesame oil.

Edamame with Chili Salt

Green edamame are actually soybeans in the pod harvested before they mature. Edamame are often sprinkled with sea salt for a quick and easy protein-filled snack. But this chili-salt adds a little more oomph and is just as yummy sprinkled over favas, broad beans or lima beans...whatever is available! Frozen edamame are fine if you can't find fresh.

PREP TIME: 5 MINUTES
COOK TIME: 5 MINUTES
MAKES: 4 TO 6 SERVINGS

2 teaspoons granulated sugar
¾ teaspoon fine sea salt
½ teaspoon crushed chili or red pepper flakes
1 lb (500 g) frozen or fresh edamame in pods

Grind the sugar and salt in a mortar with a pestle to a consistency of fine sand. Add the chili flakes and grind until fine flecks form. Stir to mix.

Bring a large pot of water to a boil over high heat. Add the edamame and cook until bright green and heated through, about 4 minutes. Drain and transfer to a large bowl. Blot dry with paper towels, then toss with the chili-salt mixture. Serve immediately. To eat, suck on the pod and use your teeth to pop the beans into your mouth.

Egg Flower Soup with English Peas and Sweet Corn

This soup is perfect for a cold, dreary day or anytime you want an easy light lunch. Depending on where you live, you may find fresh English peas and sweet corn available at the same time—they are absolutely delicious in this soup. Shelling peas isn't my favorite thing to do, so I always look out for the already-shelled English peas sometimes sold at grocery stores. To save time, or if you can't find one or the other, frozen peas or sweet corn are fine.

PREP TIME: 5 MINUTES

COOK TIME: 10 MINUTES

MAKES: 4 TO 6 SERVINGS

1 tablespoon cornstarch

3 tablespoons water

4 cups (1 liter) low-sodium
  vegetable stock

2 thin slices fresh ginger

1 large ear fresh sweet corn

½ cup (75 g) shelled English peas

2 teaspoons soy sauce

1 teaspoon Chinese cooking wine or
  dry sherry

1 teaspoon granulated sugar
  (optional)

2 eggs, lightly beaten

Sesame oil (optional)

Freshly ground white or black
  pepper

2 tablespoons finely chopped green
  onion (scallion), green and white
  parts

Stir together the cornstarch and the water in a small bowl to form a slurry. Set aside.

Heat the stock and ginger in a medium saucepan over medium heat until it starts bubbling gently, about 3 minutes.

While the stock is simmering, scrape the corn kernels from the cob. Stand the cob tip-down on your cutting board (or in the hole of a bundt pan). Use a sharp chef's knife to shave kernels off the cob with a quick downward motion. Rotate and shave off another section. Try to get as close to the cob as you can without cutting into it. Finally, scrape the cob to remove remaining kernels and flavorful milky liquid. You'll get about 1½ cups (450 g) of kernels and juice.

Add the peas and the corn kernels and liquid, followed by the soy sauce, cooking wine and sugar, if using. Continue simmering until the vegetables are tender, 1 to 2 minutes.

Stir the cornstarch mixture and pour it slowly into the saucepan, stirring the soup until it thickens and starts bubbling again.

Drizzle the eggs around the saucepan in a steady stream through a pair of chopsticks or a fork. Stir in one direction until skinny ribbons form. Remove from the heat.

Divide the soup into 4 to 6 soup bowls. Drizzle with sesame oil, if using, sprinkle with pepper and garnish with green onions.

Tip 1 lb (500 g) English pea pods will yield 1 cup of shelled peas. Shell them just before cooking: Break off the stem and pull the fibrous string down the length of the pod. Press each pod between your thumb and forefinger and push out the individual peas.

Use chopsticks or a fork to drizzle the egg into the soup in a steady stream.

Stir continuously as the egg cooks.

The egg should form short ribbons.

Grilled Vegetable Kebabs with Two Marinades

Have you ever had a mixed veggie kebab where the cherry tomatoes were shriveled and mushy but the mushrooms were still floury and raw? The simple act of color-coding and skewering one type of vegetable on one skewer solves this problem. This way, every vegetable, whether zucchini, tomato or onion, can cook to its prime without compromise. One word about choosing eggplant (aubergine) for kebabs: Try to find Japanese or Chinese eggplants. They're long and skinny, so it's easy to cut them crosswise into rounds and thread through the skewers. Plus, you don't have to play engineer to figure out the best shape and size to cut them into, as you would with a pear-shaped globe eggplant.

PREP TIME: 20 MINUTES

COOK TIME: 10 MINUTES
 (DEPENDING ON THE NUMBER OF
 BATCHES)

MAKES: 4 SERVINGS

1 medium zucchini, cut into ¾-in
 (2-cm) thick rounds

1 large red bell pepper,
 stemmed, seeded and cut into
 2-in (5-cm) squares

1 large red onion, peeled,
 quartered and cut into 1½-in
 (4-cm) petals

¾ lb (375 g) eggplant, cut into
 ¾-in (2-cm) thick slices

12 button mushrooms

12 cherry tomatoes

12 to 18 bamboo skewers, soaked
 in water for 30 minutes

½ cup (125 ml) Japanese Grilling
 Sauce or Lemongrass-Citrus
 Marinade (page 77)

Place the zucchini in a large bowl and toss with 1 to 2 tablespoons of your chosen marinade. Repeat with the remaining vegetables in separate bowls, working with one type at a time and keeping them separate.

Use 2 to 3 skewers per type of vegetable, and don't mix vegetables on any skewer. Thread the zucchini and eggplant horizontally through the slices so the cut sides will lie flat on the grill. Leave a ½-inch (1.5-cm) gap between the tomatoes, mushrooms, bell peppers and onions.

Prepare a grill for cooking over medium-hot coals or moderate heat for gas. Lightly oil the grill rack.

Grill the kebabs in two to three batches, covering if using a gas grill. Grill for 6 to 10 minutes (depending on the vegetable), turning over once, until the vegetables are tender and lightly browned. The tomatoes should be blistered and shriveled.

Transfer the skewers to a platter as they cook. Drizzle with remaining marinade

Tips Vegetables can be threaded onto skewers
1 day ahead and chilled, covered.
 • You can also broil the vegetable skewers in
2 batches on the oiled rack of a broiler pan, 4 to 6
inches from preheated broiler. Turn over once.
 • Both marinades can be made a week ahead.
Refrigerate in an airtight container.

Japanese Grilling Sauce

Tare is a general term used in Japanese for basting sauces used as a marinade or dipping sauce. Think yakitori (chicken skewers), *yakiniku* (grilled meats) and especially teriyaki sauce.

PREP TIME: 30 MINUTES
MAKES: ½ CUP (125 ML)

2 cloves garlic, smashed and peeled
Chubby 1-in (2.5-cm) knob fresh ginger, peeled and sliced
1 green onion (scallion), cut into 2-in (5-cm) pieces
½ cup (125 ml) low-sodium vegetable stock
¼ cup (60 ml) soy sauce
¼ cup (60 ml) mirin
2 tablespoons honey
1 tablespoon rice vinegar

Bring all ingredients to a boil in a medium saucepan over medium-high heat, stirring to mix. Reduce the heat to medium-low and simmer until reduced to a little more than ½ cup (125 ml), 20 to 30 minutes. Strain and discard the solids. Allow to cool.

Lemongrass-Citrus Marinade

Traditionally, this marinade uses the juice of the native Filipino lime called calamansi. Fragrant Meyer lemon is a good substitute, or you can combine orange and lime juices.

PREP TIME: 5 MINUTES
MAKES: ½ CUP (125 ML)

3 cloves garlic
Chubby 1-in (2.5-cm) knob fresh ginger, peeled and sliced
1 plump stalk lemongrass, trimmed, white part roughly chopped
1 tablespoon plus 1 teaspoon dark brown sugar
2 teaspoons fine sea salt
1 teaspoon freshly ground black pepper
¼ cup (60 ml) citrus juice (preferably 2 tablespoons lemon or lime and 2 tablespoons orange)
2 tablespoons vegetable oil
1 tablespoon rice or cider vinegar

Place the garlic, ginger and lemongrass in a small food processor and pulse until the mixture resembles confetti. Transfer to a bowl and whisk together with the sugar, salt, black pepper, citrus juice, oil and vinegar.

Thai Basil Zucchini

Thai basil pork or chicken is a standard dish served at most Thai restaurants. I've discovered that zucchini and Thai basil make a winning combination as well. If you'd like a counterpoint to the soft zucchini, mix in some chopped green beans for a crunchy texture. Most Asian markets carry Thai basil, but if you can't obtain it, substitute any kind of basil or a mixture of basil and mint for a bright, refreshing flavor. Or, if you have a green thumb, grow some in your herb garden (page 18).

PREP TIME: 10 MIN
COOK TIME: 15 MINUTES
MAKES: 4 SERVINGS

2 tablespoons vegetable oil
2 tablespoons minced garlic
½ cup (60 g) sliced shallots
1½ lbs (750 g) zucchini, quartered lengthwise and then cut crosswise into triangles
¼ teaspoon fine sea salt
4 to 6 red Thai chilies, chopped (or to taste)
2 tablespoons soy sauce
2 teaspoons coconut palm sugar or 1½ teaspoons dark brown sugar
1½ cups (40 g) packed fresh Thai basil leaves (or 1 cup/25 g Italian basil and ½ cup/15 g mint leaves)
Freshly ground black pepper

Swirl the oil into a large wok or skillet and set over medium heat until shimmering hot. Stir in the garlic and shallots and cook until aromatic, about 30 seconds.

Raise the heat to high and add the zucchini. Sprinkle in the salt. Stir and cook until the zucchini is lightly browned and translucent, 8 to 10 minutes. Cover to hasten the cooking if necessary.

Reduce the heat to medium and throw in the chilies. Add the soy sauce and sugar and stir to coat the zucchini. Stir in the basil. Continue cooking until the basil is wilted and the zucchini is done to your liking, another 30 seconds to 1 minute.

Scoop into a serving dish and sprinkle with pepper. Serve hot with steamed jasmine rice.

Tips Try to find small Thai basil leaves. If you can only find big leaves, chop or tear them up.
• If you can't find Thai chilies, substitute 1 or 2 red Serrano or Fresno chilies, cut into large slivers, with or without the seeds.

Turmeric Zucchini and Carrot Stir-Fry

Most people don't think of summer as prime stir-frying season. It is, in fact, a great time to stir-fry because of the bounty of fresh, tasty vegetables available. Don't worry, you won't suffer in front of the stove for long—stir-frying equals quick cooking. I like this combination of orange carrots and green zucchini, but just about any vegetable available in abundance at the farmers' market or grocery store will do. Try crookneck squash, green beans, okra or sweet corn in this dish, called *orak arik* in Indonesia.

PREP: 10 MINUTES
COOK: 10 MINUTES
MAKES: 4 SERVINGS

2 tablespoons vegetable oil
2 cloves garlic, minced
½ cup (60 g) chopped shallot
  or red onion
½ teaspoon ground turmeric
  powder
1½ cups (250 g) matchstick-
  cut carrots
1½ cups (250 g) matchstick-
  cut zucchini
2 large eggs, lightly beaten
½ teaspoon fine sea salt
¼ teaspoon freshly ground
  black or white pepper
2 green onions (scallions),
  green parts only, chopped
Handful of celery leaves or
  coriander leaves (cilantro),
  for garnish

Swirl the oil into a large wok or nonstick skillet and set over medium-high heat until shimmering hot. Add the garlic and shallots, followed by the turmeric. Stir and cook until the paste darkens and becomes aromatic, 1 to 2 minutes.

Add the carrots and zucchini and toss to coat with the paste. Stir and cook until soft, 2 to 3 minutes.

Pour the eggs over the vegetables slowly and cook undisturbed until they start to set, 45 seconds to 1 minute. Break up the egg into large pieces and mix into the vegetables. Sprinkle with salt and pepper, and continue to cook, stirring, until the vegetables are done to your liking. Stir in the green onions and taste, adjusting seasonings if necessary. Transfer to a serving bowl, top with the celery or coriander leaves and serve hot with steamed jasmine rice.

Stir-Fried Heirloom Tomatoes and Egg

You won't see stir-fried tomatoes and egg on Chinese restaurant menus because it's a simple dish usually only eaten at home. But many Chinese-Americans will likely have their own family recipe. Using multihued heirloom tomatoes gives this dish a modern twist, but feel free to use any fresh tomatoes you can find. Adjust the amount of sugar according to the sweetness of your tomatoes.

PREP TIME: 5 MINUTES
COOK TIME: 10 MINUTES
MAKES: 4 SERVINGS

6 large eggs
2 teaspoons sesame oil
2 tablespoons vegetable oil, divided
1 clove garlic, minced
1 green onion (scallion), chopped, white and green parts separated
1 lb (500 g) heirloom tomatoes, cut into wedges
½ teaspoon fine sea salt
¼ teaspoon granulated sugar

Beat the eggs in a medium bowl, then stir in the sesame oil.

Swirl 1 tablespoon of the vegetable oil into a large wok or nonstick skillet and set over medium-high heat until shimmering hot. Add the garlic and whites of the green onion and cook, stirring, until aromatic, about 30 seconds. Pour in the egg mixture and allow to cook undisturbed until it just begins to set at the bottom. Break up the eggs into large pieces and continue to cook, stirring, for a few more seconds, until they look like runny scrambled eggs. Transfer to a bowl and wipe out the wok.

Heat the remaining tablespoon of vegetable oil in the wok over medium-high heat until shimmering hot. Add the tomatoes and cook, stirring, until the tomatoes release their juices and their skins start to loosen, 3 to 5 minutes. Toss in the rest of the green onions. Season with salt and sugar and stir to mix. Return the eggs to the wok and stir until they are just cooked through, about 1 minute. Don't let the tomatoes turn mushy. Transfer to a bowl or platter and serve with steamed jasmine rice.

Mixed Vegetable Salad with Indonesian Peanut Sauce

This delicious salad can be eaten as a first course or a main meal. Most of the prep work involves cutting and blanching the vegetables, but it goes by quickly. Prawn crackers are the traditional accompaniment, but store-bought vegetable chips make a great vegan substitute. If you're short on time, you can turn this into a fresh salad using lettuce, spinach, cucumbers and/or carrots.

PREP TIME: 30 MINUTES
COOK TIME: 20 MINUTES
MAKES: 4 TO 6 SERVINGS

8 oz (225 g) yellow potatoes
3 cups (300 g) shredded green cabbage
3 cups (90 g) baby spinach
2 cups (200 g) bean sprouts
5 oz (300 g) green beans, cut into 2-in (5-cm) lengths
1 small seedless cucumber, cut into half-moons
2 large hard-boiled eggs, sliced into wedges
8 oz (225 g) Fried Golden Tofu (page 43) or tempeh , cut into 2-in (5-cm) cubes
1 cup (250 ml) Gourmet Indonesian Peanut Sauce (page 36)
Vegetable chips or straws, for garnish
Fried Shallots (page 26), for garnish

Cook the potatoes in boiling salted water for 20 to 25 minutes, until fork-tender. Peel and cut into 2-inch (5-cm) cubes.

Prepare a bowl or tub of ice water. Blanch the cabbage for 1 to 2 minutes, until translucent and wilted, and transfer to the ice bath. When cool, drain on kitchen towels. Set aside. Repeat with the spinach (30 seconds to 1 minute), bean sprouts (30 seconds to 1 minute) and green beans (3 to 4 minutes). (See page 41 for tips on blanching vegetables.)

Arrange the vegetables, eggs and tofu on a large platter. Serve with a bowl of Gourmet Indonesian Peanut Sauce, with the vegetable chips and Fried Shallots on small plates alongside. Each diner should pick and choose an assortment of ingredients to put on their plate. Drizzle 2 to 3 tablespoons of Gourmet Indonesian Peanut Sauce over the vegetables and top with vegetable chips and Fried Shallots. Stir everything together and enjoy!

Eggplant with Red Pepper-Tomato Sauce

My mom always uses long, slender Chinese eggplants in this dish— she says globe eggplants have skin that's tough as leather. But I think she actually just goes for what she's used to. Oh, well...we're all creatures of habit.

PREP TIME: 20 MINUTES
COOK TIME: 15 MINUTES
MAKES: 4 SERVINGS

3 tablespoons vegetable oil, divided
1 medium (1¼ lbs/550 g) purple globe
   eggplant, cut into 3 x ¾-in (7.5 x 2-cm)
   strips
2 cloves garlic, smashed and peeled
½ cup (60 g) roughly chopped shallot or red
   onion
1 red bell pepper, stemmed, seeded and
   roughly chopped
1 cup (150 g) cherry tomatoes, halved
1 teaspoon chili paste like *sambal oelek*
2 Asian (kaffir) lime leaves (optional)
½ cup (75 g) chopped white or yellow onion
½ teaspoon fine sea salt
¼ teaspoon granulated sugar

Swirl 2 tablespoons of oil into a large wok or skillet and set over medium-high heat. When shimmering hot, add the eggplant and cook, stirring, until the skin wrinkles and the flesh turns translucent and browns, 5 to 6 minutes. Transfer to a plate and set aside.

In a small food-processor, process the garlic, shallot, bell pepper and tomatoes for 30 seconds to 1 minute until they form a paste that resembles oatmeal. It will be a little watery, but you want confetti-sized bits to remain—you're not making gazpacho here!

In the same wok or skillet, swirl in the last tablespoon of oil and set over high heat. When shimmering hot, stir in the processed pepper and tomatoes, chili paste and lime leaves (if using). Fry until you can smell the red pepper and lime leaves, and most of the juices have evaporated, 4 to 6 minutes. Reduce the heat to medium, stir in the chopped onion, and simmer briefly. Add the salt and sugar and taste the sauce. Adjust the balance of flavors as needed, depending on how sweet the pepper and tomatoes are.

Simmer for another 2 to 3 minutes, until the onion is cooked but still crunchy. Add the fried eggplant strips and let them roll around in the sauce until well coated. Serve hot with steamed jasmine rice.

Tip My mom likes to steam her eggplant instead of pan-frying it in the first step of this recipe. Even easier, cover the eggplant with damp paper towels and microwave on high for 2 to 4 minutes.

Spicy Fried Okra

Infamous for its slimy texture, okra is far from everyone's favorite vegetable, but this dish just might convert you. Buy okra pods that are evenly green and about 3 to 4 inches (5 to 10 cm) long; avoid pods that look shriveled or are soft when squeezed.

PREP TIME: 10 MINUTES
COOK TIME: 5 MINUTES
MAKES: 4 SERVINGS

2 tablespoons vegetable oil

1 tablespoon minced garlic

1 tablespoon minced shallots

12 oz (350 g) fresh small okra, stems trimmed, and cut into ½-in (1.5-cm) slices on the diagonal and patted dry

¼ teaspoon fine sea salt

3 to 4 tablespoons Homemade Roasted Chili Paste (page 33)

1 teaspoon soy sauce

Swirl the oil into a large wok or skillet and set over high heat until shimmering hot. Add the garlic and shallots, followed by the okra and salt. Cook, stirring, for 2 to 3 minutes, until the okra turns bright green.

Reduce the heat to medium and add the Homemade Roasted Chili Paste and soy sauce. Stir and cook until the okra is nicely coated and crisp-tender, another 1 to 2 minutes. Serve immediately.

Tip To keep okra from getting slimy, lay pods out to dry on kitchen towel and gently pat dry with paper towels after washing, then let them sit out to dry out further. Also, cook okra hot and fast.

Eggplant "Meatball" Banh Mi Vietnamese Sandwich

The Vietnamese banh mi sandwich has taken the culinary world by storm. This eggplant "meatball" version is a refreshing change from the usual banh mi filled with meat paté or pork. The extras—sriracha mayo, pickles, veggies, and herbs—are just as important as the filling, creating a unique sandwich that's fun, flavorful, crunchy and fresh-tasting. Did I hear banh mi party?

PREP TIME: 30 MINUTES
COOK TIME: 1 HOUR 15 MINUTES
MAKES: 4 SERVINGS

Eggplant "Meatballs"

1¼ lbs (625 g) purple globe eggplant
1 teaspoon vegetable oil
1 tablespoon soy sauce
1 large egg, lightly beaten
¼ teaspoon freshly ground black pepper
2 teaspoons minced garlic
2 tablespoons finely chopped Thai or Italian basil leaves
2 tablespoons finely chopped green onion (scallion), white and green parts
1½ cups (75 g) panko breadcrumbs
Vegetable oil, for frying

Sriracha Mayonnaise

½ cup (100 g) good-quality mayonnaise
1 to 2 tablespoons sriracha or Spicy Miso Dip (page 120)
1 teaspoon freshly squeezed lemon or lime juice
¼ teaspoon soy sauce

Sandwiches

Four (10-in/25-cm-long) mini baguettes or bollilos (Mexican buns) (you can also cut two baguettes into four 10-in/25-cm sections)
½ cup (75 g) Quick Vinegar Daikon and Carrot Pickles (page 40), drained
½ cup (50 g) thinly sliced cucumbers or radishes
¼ cup (5 g) fresh coriander (cilantro) sprigs
1 jalapeño or Fresno chili cut into slices (optional)

Preheat oven to 350°F (180°C).

Place the eggplant on a rimmed baking sheet, brush with the oil, and prick all over with a fork. Roast for about 1 hour, until the eggplant skin is grayish and wrinkly and the flesh is tender (poke with a fork to test). Remove from the oven and allow to rest until cool enough to handle.

Halve the eggplant lengthwise and scoop out the flesh onto a cutting board, discarding the skin. Chop with a knife until it turns mushy. Combine the chopped eggplant, soy sauce, egg, pepper, garlic, basil, green onion and panko in a large bowl. Mix together gently with a wooden spoon until well combined.

If making the meatball mixture ahead, place in a sealed container and refrigerate for up to one day.

Spray a large rimmed baking sheet with cooking spray. Scoop up 1 tablespoon of the eggplant mixture at a time and form into golf-ball-sized rounds. Roll tightly and place on the baking sheet 1 inch apart. You should have about 20 to 24 "meatballs." Cover with plastic wrap and refrigerate for up to 2 hours.

Pour 1 inch (2.5 cm) of oil into a large saucepan or cast-iron skillet and set over medium-high heat until the temperature reaches 375°F (190°C) on a deep-fry thermometer. Working in small batches, gently lower the "meatballs" into the hot oil, taking care not to overcrowd the pan. Fry until golden brown on the bottom, about 2 minutes. Turn with a spatula and fry the other side until golden brown, another 2 minutes or so.

Drain on a rack over a baking sheet or paper towel-lined plate. Raise the heat to bring the oil back up to temp and repeat until all the "meatballs" are cooked.

When you're ready to make the sandwiches, whisk together the mayonnaise, sriracha sauce, lemon juice and soy sauce in a small bowl to make the Sriracha Mayonnaise.

Split each baguette in half lengthwise. Scrape out enough soft crumbs from each half to leave a ½-in (1.5-cm) thick shell. Spread Sriracha Mayonnaise over both halves. Arrange 4 to 5 meatballs in the well on the bottom half, followed by pickles, cucumbers, coriander and jalapeños (if using). Press the baguette halves together. Slice in half and serve.

Cambodian Sweet Soy Noodles with Pickles

There's a tiny hole-in-the-wall Cambodian restaurant in Seattle's International District called Phnom Penh that I've been going to since my college days. One of my favorite dishes is called "Battambang Noodles," named after the major city in Northwest Cambodia. Phnom Penh jazzes up this simple dried noodle dish with a mélange of flavors: Sweet soy sauce, salty preserved radish and sour cucumber pickles. And except for the brininess of the ground dried shrimp, I believe my version is a close approximation.

PREP TIME: 20 MINUTES
COOK TIME: 5 MINUTES
MAKES: 4 SERVINGS

1 lb (500 g) fresh or 8 oz (250 g) dried thin rice noodles (*banh pho*, page 17)
3 tablespoons vegetable oil
2 large cloves garlic, smashed and peeled
½ teaspoon fine sea salt

Sweet Soy Sauce

2 tablespoons soy sauce
1 tablespoon water
2 tablespoons coconut palm sugar or 1 to 1½ tablespoons dark brown sugar

Toppings

½ cup (75 g) assorted pickles (celery, fennel, cucumber)
8 oz (250 g) Broiled Tofu, store-bought or homemade (page 42), cut into bite-sized pieces
2 cups (200 g) bean sprouts, blanched for 30 seconds to 1 minute
4 large hard-boiled eggs, chopped (optional)
2 tablespoons preserved radish, soaked, drained and chopped (optional)
2 tablespoons Microwaved Crispy Garlic Bits (page 25)
¼ cup (30 g) crushed roasted peanuts

Garnishes

2 tablespoons chopped green onion (scallion), green parts only
1 cup (25 g) assorted herbs plucked off their stems (Thai or Italian basil, cilantro, parsley)
1 large lime, quartered
Soy sauce
Chili paste such as *sambal oelek*

Tip You can easily add meat to this dish for your meat-loving family or friends. Simply marinate chicken, beef or pork in one of the marinades used for the Broiled Tofu (page 42) and cook as desired.

To make the Sweet Soy Sauce, combine the soy sauce, water and palm sugar in a small microwave-safe bowl. Microwave on medium for 1 minute, then stir until the sugar dissolves.

Bring a large pot of water to a rolling boil. If using fresh noodles, dip them in the boiling water for about 1 minute (or prepare according to package directions). Stir to loosen and unravel the strands. (If using dried noodles, submerge them in the boiling water and turn off the heat. Stir to loosen and unravel them. When noodles are completely limp, test for doneness. They should be cooked through but still al dente, 6 to 8 minutes. Pay attention, because they'll turn mushy if overcooked.) Drain and rinse noodles under cold running water. Drain again in a colander over the sink to dry off the noodles as much as possible.

Swirl the oil into a large wok or skillet and set over medium heat until shimmering hot. Swish the garlic around in the oil until golden to flavor the oil, 4 to 5 minutes. Remove and discard.

Toss the cooked noodles in the oil for a few seconds, then pour the Sweet Soy Sauce over the noodles and toss until well coated. Sprinkle with the salt and mix well. Remove the noodles from the heat and divide among 4 large bowls.

To serve, top each bowl of noodles with a fourth of the pickles, tofu, bean sprouts, eggs (if using), preserved radish (if using), Microwaved Crispy Garlic Bits and peanuts. Serve immediately with garnishes alongside in small dishes.

Summer Herb Rice Salad

I love eating this flavorful rice salad for a light lunch during summer. Unless you're a stickler for tradition, you can add whatever herbs you have growing in your garden or that you picked up at the farmers' market. Feel free to choose between coriander leaf (cilantro) and parsley; Italian basil and Thai basil. Don't throw in the herbs while the rice is still warm, they will blacken. If you're impatient, wait till it cools down to at least room temperature. To turn this dish into a more complete meal, toss in shredded cooked carrots or green beans, and top with shredded omelet or baked tofu or tempeh.

PREP TIME: 25 MINUTES + 10 MINUTES SITTING TIME
COOK TIME: 45 MINUTES
MAKES: 4 SERVINGS

2 cups (400 g) uncooked wild rice blend (I recommend Lundberg or Della brand)
¼ cup (60 ml) lime juice
2 teaspoons fine sea salt
2 teaspoons granulated sugar
½ teaspoon freshly ground black pepper
½ cup (10 g) loosely packed Thai or Italian basil leaves, finely sliced
½ cup (10 g) loosely packed mint leaves, finely sliced
½ cup (10 g) loosely packed coriander leaves (cilantro), finely sliced
4 Asian (kaffir) lime leaves, central ribs removed, finely sliced (optional), or 1 to 2 teaspoons lime zest
½ cup (60 g) thinly sliced shallot, soaked in water to tame its bite
2 plump stalks lemongrass, trimmed and minced (2 to 3 tablespoons total)
1 cup (60 g) Toasted Coconut Flakes (page 25)
2 to 3 Thai chilies, thinly sliced (optional)
2 tablespoons Microwaved Crispy Garlic Bits (page 25), for garnish
2 tablespoons Fried Shallots (page 26), for garnish
2 tablespoons crushed roasted peanuts, for garnish
Sliced tomatoes or cucumbers, for serving

Cook the wild rice blend according to the package directions (it should yield about 5 cups of cooked rice). Chill for 2 hours.

Whisk together the lime juice, salt, sugar and pepper in a large serving bowl. Stir in the chilled cooked rice, basil, mint, coriander leaves, lime leaves (if using), shallots, lemongrass, Toasted Coconut Flakes and Thai chilies (if using). Toss, then let stand for 10 minutes to allow the flavors to meld. Sprinkle with the Microwaved Crispy Garlic Bits, Fried Shallots and crushed peanuts. Serve with the sliced cucumbers or tomatoes.

Tips This recipe is easily multiplied to serve a crowd.
• Instead of a wild rice blend, try using a fluffy rice like basmati or jasmine rice. Don't use Japanese or arborio rice, however; they are too sticky.

Buckwheat Noodles and Shoyu Dipping Sauce

"Zaru soba" is the Japanese name for this dish of cold buckwheat noodles (soba) served in a bamboo basket (zaru). The noodles are served with simple accompaniments like toasted nori seaweed, daikon radish, wasabi and sometimes tempura. Here, I've added zucchini cut into fine threads to blend with the noodles. Carrots, radishes, and any kind of summer squash would be wonderful too. Made with soy sauce (shoyu), mirin and dashi, the versatile sauce is not just perfect for dipping noodles and tempura—it can also be used to season vegetables and tofu.

PREP TIME: 20 MINUTES + MELDING TIME
COOK: 10 MINUTES
MAKES: 4 SERVINGS

Dipping Sauce

¼ cup (60 ml) mirin

1 tablespoon granulated sugar (or to taste)

¼ cup (60 ml) soy sauce

1½ to 2 cups (375 to 500 ml) Dashi Seaweed Stock (page 29)

5 oz (150 g) zucchini, cut into threads

One 12-oz (350-g) package dried soba

½ cup (5 g) shredded or crumbled toasted nori or Kale "Chips" (page 26)

2 tablespoons finely chopped green onion (scallion), green and white parts

Wasabi paste (optional)

Tips Feel free to add more or less dashi according to your taste. Adding more dashi than the standard 3:1 ratio tames the saltiness a little.

• The sauce recipe is easily multiplied, so you can store it in the refrigerator for a few weeks.

• The concentrate can also be diluted with 4 or 5 parts water to make a soup base for another meal.

To make the Dipping Sauce, prepare a concentrate by warming the mirin in a small saucepan over low heat until it starts to bubble. (This will remove most of the alcohol.) Stir in the sugar until it dissolves. Pour in the soy sauce and continue to stir until well mixed. Remove from the heat and refrigerate for 2 to 3 hours (overnight is fine) so the flavors can meld.

Combine the concentrate with 1½ cups (375 ml) of the dashi. Stir and taste. If it's too salty, add up to ½ cup (125 ml) more dashi to dilute it. It should taste a little salty on its own, because you'll be dipping the bland noodles into it.

Bring a large pot of water to a rolling boil over high heat. Place the zucchini threads in a large fine-mesh sieve or spider and dunk it in the hot water for 15 to 30 seconds, until the threads go limp. Rinse under cold running water until cool and set aside.

Next, add the dried soba to the same pot in a circular motion, separating the noodles around the pot. Stir occasionally so they don't stick. Cook until al dente, 3 to 5 minutes. Don't overcook soba noodles, or they'll be gummy! Drain the noodles into a colander and rinse under cold running water to remove excess starch.

Divide the noodles among 4 serving plates. Pour about ⅓ cup (85 ml) Dipping Sauce into 4 individual small bowls or cups. Scatter the nori and zucchini threads on top of the noodles and serve with the green onions and wasabi (if using) in small dishes alongside. To eat, stir as much green onions and wasabi into your bowl of dipping sauce as you like. dip the noodles into the sauce and enjoy!

Crispy Noodles with Savory Vegetables

This Hong Kong-style dish, which is very popular at Chinese restaurants, usually comprises one big crispy noodle cake topped with chicken or seafood in a light sauce. I decided to make noodle nests that can be easily divided among diners—ideal for serving kids. See the sidebar for the good old-fashioned way of making a noodle cake. If you can't find dried Chinese noodles, you can also use instant ramen (discard the seasoning packets). And if you're lucky enough to find parboiled "Hong Kong-Style Pan-Fried Noodles" in the refrigerated section of the Asian market, all you need to do is dip them briefly in boiling water, drain them, and toss with sesame oil to prevent sticking.

PREP TIME: 15 MINUTES
COOK TIME: 25 MINUTES
MAKES: 4 TO 6 SERVINGS

8 to 10 oz (250 to 325 g) dried thin Chinese egg noodles (sometimes labeled *chuka soba*), or 16 oz (500 g) fresh Hong Kong–style pan-fried noodles

2 teaspoons sesame oil

2 tablespoons vegetable oil, for brushing

2 tablespoons miso (optional; increase salt or soy sauce if not using)

1½ teaspoons granulated sugar

3 tablespoons soy sauce

1½ cups (375 ml) low-sodium vegetable stock

1½ tablespoons cornstarch

½ cup (125 ml) water

1 tablespoon oil

2 tablespoons minced garlic

¾ cup (115 g) sliced sweet onion

1 cup (175 g) sliced red bell pepper

3 cups (180 g) chopped baby bok choy or Chinese cabbage, hard ribs and leaves separated

2 cups (180 g) broccoli florets, blanched for 1 minute

5 oz (150 g) carrots, sliced on the diagonal, blanched for 1 minute

2 oz (40 g) green onions (scallions), green and white parts, cut into 2-in (5-cm) pieces

½ teaspoon freshly ground black pepper

Bring a large pot of water to a rolling boil over high heat. Cook the noodles for 2 minutes, or 1 minute less than the package directions, stirring to unravel the strands. Drain in a colander and rinse with cold running water to stop them cooking. Separate the strands and transfer to a bowl. Drizzle with 2 teaspoons sesame oil and toss to prevent sticking.

Preheat oven to 400°F (205°F). Brush two 8-cup muffin pans liberally with oil. Divide the noodles into 16 portions, pulling, breaking or cutting if necessary, and push one portion into each muffin cup. It's okay if the noodles spill over, as they will shrink a bit. Brush the noodles liberally with oil. Bake for 18 to 20 minutes, until the noodles are crispy and golden brown. Keep warm in a low (200°F/100°C) oven. (The noodles can also be stored in an airtight container for up to 2 days.)

Stir together the miso (if using), sugar, soy sauce and stock in a medium bowl. Combine the cornstarch and water in a separate small bowl and stir to blend. Set both aside.

Swirl the 1 tablespoon oil into a large wok or skillet and set over medium-high heat until shimmering hot. Add the garlic and onions and cook, stirring, until aromatic, 30 seconds to 1 minute. Add the red pepper and bok choy ribs. Continue to stir and cook for 1 minute, then add the broccoli and carrot. Continue to cook, stirring, for 1 more minute, then add the bok choy leaves and the miso mixture. Stir to combine, then reduce the heat to medium, cover and cook until the vegetables are cooked to your liking, about 1 minute. Taste and adjust seasonings as needed.

Raise the heat to high. Stir the cornstarch mixture and pour into the wok. Bring to a boil, stirring, until the sauce reaches a gravy consistency, about 30 seconds. Add more stock or water if it's too thick. Add the green onions, toss one final time and remove from the heat.

Divide the noodle nests among 4 (or more) individual plates. Spoon the vegetables and sauce over the noodles. Sprinkle with pepper and serve immediately.

How to Make Noodle Cakes

These instructions will make 2 large noodle cakes. Cook the noodles as directed on the opposite page and divide them into 2 portions.

Swirl 1 tablespoon oil into a medium nonstick or cast-iron skillet to cover the entire surface and set over medium heat. When shimmering hot, pile one portion of the noodles into the skillet and pat down into a round cake, smoothing the edges.

Cook for about 5 minutes, scraping the bottom occasionally with a spatula to prevent sticking, until noodles are golden brown and crispy.

Place a plate on top of the skillet and invert. Return the skillet to the heat and swirl in 1 more tablespoon oil, then slide the cake back in and cook the other side, another 5 minutes or so.

Remove from the skillet and keep warm in a low (200°F/100°C) oven. Repeat with the remaining noodles.

To serve, place the 2 noodle cakes on a large serving platter and spoon the vegetables and sauce on top. Sprinkle with pepper and serve immediately.

Tips Many other summer vegetables would taste great in this dish—squash, sugar snap peas, tomatoes. Let whatever you find at the farmers' market guide you.

• Use eggless wheat noodles for a vegan version of this dish.

AUTUMN RECIPES

Of the four seasons, autumn has the greatest possibilities. During the shoulder season straddling September and October, the late summer and early autumn bounty co-mingles along grocery store aisles and at farmers' market stands. This juxtaposition of produce can lead to exciting culinary creations if you let it.

It's also time for last-minute canning and jamming to capture the essence of summer—perhaps some plum jam or pickled green beans that will keep you going through the depths of winter. Or, head to the beach or a nearby meadow for one final picnic before you send your picnic basket to the back of the closet.

The many Indian summer days of early autumn soften the blow of letting summer go. I might make a simple dish requiring minimal cooking, like Ice-Cold Ko-

Chinese Mushroom Buns (page 98)

Scooping rice into dumpling skins to make Sticky Rice Siu Mai Dumplings (page 100)

rean Buckwheat Noodles, and I'll enjoy it guilt-free because pears are already in season.

I'll also mix and match sweet corn with potatoes for Curried Vegetable Turnovers or pair the season's first kabocha (a Japanese winter squash) with peas in a simple braised dish.

Apples are in high season during autumn, too. Some varieties are ready for picking as

STARTERS & SNACKS

Green Apple Salad with
Tangy Thai Dressing

Butternut Squash
Potstickers

Curried Vegetable Turnovers

Chinese Mushroom Buns

Sticky Rice
Siu Mai Dumplings

FAMILY-STYLE DISHES

Salt and Pepper
Green Beans

Mixed Vegetables
Yellow Curry

Adobo Ratatouille

Stuffed Cabbage Parcels

Red and Golden Beets
in Green Curry

Cherry Tomatoes
Simmered with Tofu

General Tso's Eggplant

ALL-IN-ONE MEALS

Sweet Potato Rice Stew

Stir-Fried
Cellophane Noodles

Vegetable and
Egg Donburi Rice Bowl

Ice-Cold Korean
Buckwheat Noodles

Mushu Vegetable
"Burritos"

early as September, depending on where you live. Before summer tomatoes disappear for good, I'll make Green Apple Salad with Tangy Thai Dressing.

As November creeps up, I know without a doubt that autumn is here. I can smell it: Brisk, crisp air. Musty, earthy decaying leaves. The smoky, woodsy burning fireplace. Cinnamon-spiked pie in the oven signaling the impending arrival of the holidays.

I can see it: Tree crowns turning red, yellow and gold. Sidewalks littered with fallen leaves begging to be trampled. And I know it's time to pull out the slow cooker for Adobo Ratatouille and save leftover cooked rice to make Sweet Potato Rice Stew.

Stir-Fried Cellophane Noodles (page 110)

Green Apple Salad with Tangy Thai Dressing

Based on the popular Thai papaya salad (*som tum*), this refreshing salad has a delightful balance of sweet, salty and sour. Like it sweeter? Add more sugar. Not tart enough? A few more squirts of lime juice will do it. Feel free to tweak the recipe to your liking. It can be hard to find fresh, flavorful tomatoes when apples are in season; leave them out if you prefer.

PREP TIME: 20 MINUTES
MAKES: 4 SERVINGS

2 tart, firm green apples, like Granny Smith

1 plump clove garlic

2 Thai or Serrano chilies (seeded if desired)

4 teaspoons coconut palm sugar or 3 teaspoons light brown sugar

2 tablespoons roasted peanuts, divided

6 cherry tomatoes

4 teaspoons Vegan "Fish" Sauce (page 35) or soy sauce

2 tablespoons freshly squeezed lime juice

Iceberg or butter lettuce, for serving (optional)

Shred the apples with a matchstick slicer, or cut them into matchsticks by hand (peel them if you prefer). You should have about 2 cups. Soak in a bowl of salted water while you prepare the dressing.

To make the dressing, grind the garlic, chilies and sugar with a mortar and pestle until they form a paste. Add 1 tablespoon of the peanuts and grind into tiny pieces. Then add the cherry tomatoes and grind a few times just to bruise the tomatoes and release some juices. Stir in the Vegan "Fish" Sauce and lime juice. Taste and adjust seasonings as needed.

Drain the apple and place in a lint-free dish towel. Wring gently to remove excess water.

If your mortar is big enough, add the apple. If not, transfer the dressing to a serving bowl. Add the apple and half of the remaining peanuts, and toss well to mix. Sprinkle with the rest of the peanuts and serve immediately, with lettuce leaves on the side to scoop up the salad if desired.

Tips You can use a sweet-tart apple variety like Fuji or Pink Lady. Just be sure to use firm-fleshed apples, or they'll turn mushy when you shred them.

• If you're even more adventurous, semi-ripe mangoes or pineapple would taste great in this salad, as would rutabaga, jicama, or kohlrabi.

Butternut Squash Potstickers

With its glossy, dark tan skin, the baby-sized Honeynut butternut squash is a new addition to the market. I like them because they're cute and have a honey-sweet flavor. If you can't find any, use regular butternut squash, or any other winter squash like delicata, sugar pumpkin or acorn. You'll probably end up with more squash purée than you need for this recipe (small squashes are hard to come by), but you can save it for making soup or baby food—or freeze it to make more potstickers! If you're keen on convenience, canned pumpkin purée is a quick and easy option.

PREP TIME: 20 MINUTES
COOK TIME: 40 MINUTES
MAKES: 4 TO 6 SERVINGS (ABOUT 24 POTSTICKERS)

1 small (12 oz/350 g) Honeynut butternut squash

2 teaspoons soy sauce

¼ teaspoon freshly ground black pepper

1 teaspoon sesame oil

½ cup (65 g) frozen peas and/or carrots

3 tablespoons finely chopped green onion (scallion)

2 teaspoons grated fresh ginger

25 round dumpling wrappers

Vegetable oil, for pan-frying

Spicy Soy Dipping Sauce (page 37)

Tips Potstickers freeze well. Follow the directions on page 101.
• The dipping sauce can be made up to 1 day ahead, but wait till the last minute to garnish with ginger, green onions and sesame seeds (from the recipe on page 37).

Preheat oven to 375°F (190°C). Halve the squash, scoop out the seeds and stringy bits and place the halves cut side down on a greased baking sheet. Roast until tender, 20 to 30 minutes, and allow to cool.

Scoop out the flesh from the skin into a large bowl, discarding the skin. Mash with a potato masher or a fork until smooth.

Measure about 1 cup purée, setting aside any extra for future use. Mix in the soy sauce, black pepper, sesame oil, vegetables, green onions and ginger. Taste and adjust seasonings as needed.

To assemble the potstickers, set up your work station: stack the wrappers in one corner of your work surface and cover with a damp cloth so they don't dry out. Line a baking sheet with parchment paper, and fill a small bowl with water.

Peel off one wrapper and hold it flat in your left (or non-dominant) hand. Place 1 scant tablespoon of filling in the middle. Moisten the edges with your fingertip and fold to make a half-moon shape. With your thumb and index finger, make a row of pleats from left to right. Press together all the pleats to seal, making sure that the filling doesn't ooze out, and place seam-side-up on the baking sheet. Repeat with the remaining wrappers and filling.

Swirl 2 tablespoons vegetable oil into the bottom of a large nonstick or cast iron skillet to coat evenly. Set over medium heat until shimmering hot. Arrange about 10 potstickers (or however many fit without crowding) in a single layer seam-side up in the skillet and cook until the bottoms start to brown, 1 to 2 minutes. Shake the skillet periodically to make sure they don't stick. Carefully pour in about ¼ cup (60 ml) water to reach ¼ inch (0.5 cm) in depth and cover with a tight-fitting lid. Reduce the heat to medium-low and steam for 4 to 5 minutes, or until most of the liquid has evaporated and the wrappers are translucent. Loosen the potstickers gently with a spatula and transfer them to a serving dish. They should be crisp and golden brown on the bottom. Wipe out the skillet to remove any remaining water and repeat until all the potstickers are cooked.

Serve immediately with Spicy Soy Dipping Sauce alongside.

Curried Vegetable Turnovers

Growing up in Singapore, I loved to eat these savory turnovers, locally called curry puffs. They were (and still are) sold everywhere from school canteens to snack shops across the island. One family even built a food empire on chicken curry puffs! Traditional turnovers are encased in short-crust pastry and deep-fried. But I prefer this baked puff-pastry version (especially if I'm making them).

PREP TIME: 30 MINUTES

COOK TIME: 30 MINUTES

MAKES: 4 TO 6 SERVINGS (12 TURNOVERS)

2 tablespoons vegetable oil

1 clove garlic, minced

2 tablespoons chopped shallots or red onion

2 teaspoons Yellow Curry Powder (page 31)

8 oz (250 g) yellow potatoes, peeled and chopped into ¼-in (5-mm) dice

⅓ cup (15 g) diced carrot

¼ cup (60 g) diced red bell pepper

⅓ cup (85 ml) water

1 teaspoon fine sea salt

½ teaspoon granulated sugar

¼ teaspoon freshly ground black pepper

One 1-lb (500 g) box puff pastry (preferably all-butter), defrosted according to package directions

1 large egg, lightly beaten

1 tablespoon milk

Swirl the oil into a large wok or skillet and set over medium high heat until shimmering hot. Fry the garlic and shallots until aromatic, about 30 seconds. Add the Yellow Curry Powder and fry until fragrant and the shallots are well coated, another 1 minute or so.

Add the potatoes, carrots and bell peppers and mix well. Pour in the water and season with the salt, sugar and black pepper. Stir to combine, then cover and reduce heat to medium-low. Cook for 8 to 10 minutes, until the potatoes are tender. Stir occasionally, adding more water if the vegetables start sticking to the bottom of the pan. Taste and adjust seasonings if you desire, then set aside to cool. The filling can be made ahead and refrigerated for up to 2 days.

When the filling is completely cool, start assembling the turnovers.

Preheat oven to 400°F (205°C). Prepare your work station: Line a baking sheet with parchment; mix the egg and milk together in a small bowl; dust your work surface with flour.

Work with one pastry sheet at a time. Roll out the dough to make a 10 x 10-in (25 x 25-cm) square, ⅛-in (3-mm) thick. Use a small bowl to cut out four circles about 4 or 5 inches (10 or 12 cm) in diameter. Gather the scraps into a ball, reroll and cut out 2 more circles. Repeat with the second pastry sheet.

Place 1 tablespoon of filling in the center of each circle, leaving a ½-inch (1.5-cm) border around the edges. Brush the edge of the border with the egg mixture and fold the pastry over the filling to make a half-moon. Press along the edge with fork tines to seal and place the turnover on the baking sheet. Repeat.

Brush the top of each turnover with the egg mixture. Bake for 15 to 20 minutes until the pastry is golden brown. Wait at least 5 minutes before serving.

Tips Traditionally, curry puffs are a half-moon shape. But my recipe tester Laura McCarthy prefers to cut the pastry into 12 equal squares and fold each turnover into a triangle.

• To be extra fancy, slice 2 hard-boiled eggs crosswise into sixths and nestle one slice in the filling before sealing each turnover.

• Don't just stick to carrots and red peppers. Use corn, peas, celery—whatever veggies you have on hand.

• Baked turnovers can be refrigerated for a few days and reheated in a warm (300°F/150°C) oven for 15 minutes.

Chinese Mushroom Buns

These tasty snacks are a riff on the popular baked barbecued pork buns (*char siu bao*). In my vegan version, I cook the mushroom filling with the same seasonings as barbecued pork and use store-bought dough to simplify the prep work as much as possible. The dough might seem fiddly to work with, but the convenience of not having to make my own dough far outweighs this drawback. Plus, there is little compromise on taste.

PREP TIME: 30 MINUTES

COOK TIME: 25 MINUTES

MAKES: 16 BUNS

1 tablespoon granulated sugar

1 teaspoon Chinese Five-Spice Powder (page 31)

3 tablespoons low-sodium vegetable stock

2 tablespoons soy sauce

1 tablespoon Chinese cooking wine or dry sherry

2 teaspoons sesame oil

1½ tablespoons cornstarch

¼ cup (60 ml) water

2 tablespoons vegetable oil

1 tablespoon minced garlic

½ cup (75 g) finely chopped shallots or red onion

7 cups (500 g) chopped white or brown mushrooms

¼ teaspoon fine sea salt

¼ teaspoon freshly ground black pepper

6 tablespoons chopped green onion (scallion), green and white parts separated

Two 8-oz (225-g) tubes crescent rolls

2 tablespoons honey

1 tablespoon warm water

Make the sauce by whisking together the sugar, Five-Spice Powder, vegetable stock, soy sauce, cooking wine and sesame oil in a small bowl. In a separate bowl, stir the cornstarch and water together.

Swirl the vegetable oil into a large wok or skillet and set over medium-high heat. Add the garlic and shallots and cook, stirring, until aromatic and translucent, 1 to 2 minutes. Add the mushrooms and season with salt and pepper. Continue to stir and cook until the mushrooms start to release their juices, 2 to 3 minutes.

Add the white parts of the green onions, followed by the sauce, and stir and cook until the mixture starts to bubble. Reduce the heat to medium and continue to cook, stirring, until the mushrooms are cooked through, another 5 to 6 minutes. Taste a mushroom to test; it shouldn't leave a floury taste in your mouth.

Stir the cornstarch mixture, then drizzle over the mushrooms. Stir until the filling becomes thick and glossy. Fold in the green parts of the green onions. You should have about 1¾ cups filling.

Spread the filling out on two large platters. When cool, refrigerate uncovered until cold. Taste and adjust the seasonings as needed. The filling can be refrigerated in a sealed container for up to 2 days.

To assemble the buns, flour a work surface. Remove a log of dough from one tube and roll with your fingertips to seal the perforated seams. Cut the log in half crosswise to yield 2 pieces. Then cut each half in half, making 4 pieces. Finally, cut each of these in half to yield 8 pieces. Repeat with the second tube; you should have 16 (approximately 1-inch/2.5-cm) discs in total.

Preheat oven to 350°F (180°C).

Unravel each disc and roll into a ball. With a rolling pin, roll the dough into a 3-inch (7.5-cm) circle from the middle out. If possible, leave a "belly," making the wrapper thicker in the middle than around the edges, in order to help support the weight of the filling. Pull and stretch the circle if you have to, but don't overwork the dough or it will become too elastic.

Scoop about 2 teaspoons of the filling into the middle of the circle, leaving a ½-inch (1-cm) border. Pinch two edges of the dough together at the midpoint. Then pinch and pleat all around while pushing the filling down. Finally, pinch and twist to seal the bun with a "topknot." Place the bun seam-side down on a greased sheet pan. Repeat until all the buns are assembled (you may have filling left over).

Stir together the honey and warm water, and brush over the buns thickly.

Bake for 16 to 20 minutes, until the buns are golden brown and shiny. Serve warm or at room temperature.

Tip Wrap any leftover filling in Swiss Chard Brown Rice Sushi Hand Rolls (page 132) to make rice balls, or in Crispy Spring Rolls (page 50) and bake or deep-fry.

Sticky Rice Siu Mai Dumplings

If you've had dim sum at a restaurant, then you've probably had a version of these dumplings called *siu mai, shiu mai,* or *shao mai,* depending who you ask. Here's a vegan version made with sticky (glutinous) rice and mushrooms. Instead of water chestnuts, I've added chestnuts for a hint of sweetness and nuttiness, as well as seasonality.

PREP TIME: 45 MINUTES
COOK TIME: 30 MINUTES
**MAKES: 8 TO 10 SERVINGS
   (48 DUMPLINGS)**

1 cup (200 g) uncooked sticky (glutinous) rice (also called *malagkit*), soaked for at least 3 hours, preferably overnight

1 tablespoon vegetable oil, plus additional oil for brushing

¼ cup (40 g) finely chopped yellow onion

2 to 3 green onions (scallions), chopped to yield 2 tablespoons white parts, 4 tablespoons green parts, kept separate

1 cup (75 g) diced button mushrooms

½ teaspoon fine sea salt

2 teaspoons soy sauce

1 teaspoon sesame oil

½ cup (60 g) cooked whole chestnuts (about 10), peeled and chopped

½ cup (65 g) frozen peas or carrots, plus more, for garnish

50 thin dumpling wrappers (round or square)

Cook the soaked sticky rice according to package directions. (You can also cook it in the microwave, my preferred method: Place the rice in a large microwave-safe bowl and add 1 cup plus 2 tablespoons water. Cover with a damp paper towel and cook for 3 minutes. Stir, then cook for another 3 to 5 minutes, checking every minute, until the rice is completely translucent and tender. Cooking time will depend on the wattage of your microwave.) If the rice still seems dry, sprinkle with 1 to 2 tablespoons water and cover with a damp towel. Set rice aside.

Swirl 1 tablespoon of the vegetable oil into a large wok and set over medium heat until shimmering hot. Add the yellow onions and the white parts of the green onions and fry until aromatic, 30 seconds to 1 minute. Add the mushrooms and salt and cook, stirring, for 2 to 3 minutes, until they are soft and release their juices. Add the soy sauce, sesame oil, and the green parts of the green onions, then stir in the cooked rice, chestnuts, and peas. Remove from the heat and mix well. Taste and adjust seasonings as needed.

Tips Uncooked dumplings freeze well. Arrange them on a baking sheet 1 in (2.5 cm) apart and freeze for at least 1 hour, then transfer into zip-top freezer bags. Steam frozen dumplings as usual but add 3 or 4 minutes to the cooking time.

• Sticky rice is available at many Asian markets, Don't buy Japanese-style "sticky rice" which is japonica short-grain rice. Specialty super-markets sell purple glutinous rice in the bulk section or under brands like Lundberg and Della. This whole-grain rice is heartier and sweeter, but works in a pinch.

• This recipe can easily be halved; however, I recom-mend using 1 cup (200 g) of sticky rice so that it cooks evenly. Steep the leftover rice in sweetened coconut milk and top with fruit for a simple dessert.

To assemble the dumplings, set up your work station: place the filling in a bowl; cover the dumpling wrappers with a damp towel to prevent them from drying out, Line the steamer tray or basket with parchment or brush with veg-etable oil to prevent sticking. Pour 2 to 3 inches (5 to 7.5 cm) of water into the steamer, then cover and bring to a boil over medium-high heat.

Peel off one wrapper and place it in your left (or non-dominant) palm. Scoop 1 heaping tablespoon of filling into the middle, pressing down gently. Curl your palm around the wrapper so it naturally gathers around the filling into an open purse. Make pleats while rotating the dumpling to close the opening. Hold the wrapper closed as you stand the dumpling onto your work surface, flattening the bottom so that it sits upright. Position a pea or carrot on top as garnish and place it in the steamer basket. Repeat until basket is full, posi-tioning dumplings about 1 inch (2.5 cm) apart and brushing the tops with oil to prevent them from drying out.

When the steamer basket is full, reduce the heat to medium and carefully lift the steamer lid away from you. Insert the basket and steam the dumplings for 6 to 7 minutes, or until the wrappers turn translucent. (See page 14 for steaming tips.) Continue to assemble dumplings while this batch is cooking.

Transfer the cooked dumplings to a large platter and cover with foil (shiny side down) so they stay warm while you steam the rest.

Salt and Pepper Green Beans

The pepper in this dish actually refers to the Sichuan peppercorns, which add a different kind of heat to foods. But you can substitute with another flavorful peppercorn if you wish.

PREP TIME: 10 MINUTES
COOK TIME: 10 MINUTES
MAKES: 4 SERVINGS

1 teaspoon fine sea salt
1 teaspoon Five-Spice Powder (page 31)
1 teaspoon Sichuan peppercorns or
   other flavorful peppercorns like
   Tellicherry black pepper
1½ tablespoons cornstarch
1 tablespoon all-purpose flour
4 tablespoons water
1 lb (500 g) green beans, trimmed
Vegetable oil, for frying
2 teaspoons minced garlic

Place the salt, Five-Spice Powder and Sichuan peppercorns in a mortar and pound until crushed. Set aside.

In a medium bowl, stir together the cornstarch, flour and water to make a very thin batter. Add the green beans and toss to coat.

Pour enough oil into a large wok or skillet to reach a depth of 1 inch (2.5 cm) and set over medium-high heat until shimmering hot. Pick up a few green beans at a time with tongs or chopsticks, letting excess batter run off, and slip into the hot oil. Fry beans in 2 to 3 batches, taking care to separate and turn them occasionally, until they are shriveled, blistered, and brown in spots, 2 to 4 minutes. Remove with a slotted spoon and drain on a plate lined with paper towels or rack set over a baking sheet. Keep warm in a low (200°F/100°C) oven. Repeat until all green beans are fried.

Wipe out your wok, leaving about 1 tablespoon of oil and set over medium heat. Fry the garlic until aromatic, about 30 seconds. Stir in the pounded spices and cook until aromatic, about 30 seconds. Return the green beans to the wok and toss to coat with seasonings. Serve immediately with steamed jasmine rice.

Broiling the Green Beans

When preparing the beans, add 1 teaspoon of oil to the cornstarch, flour, and water mixture. Set an oven rack just under the heating element and preheat broiler to high. Spread green beans out on an oiled broiler pan. Broil for about 2 minutes. Flip, then broil for another 1 minute or until blistered, shriveled, and brown in spots. Follow the rest of the recipe directions.

Tip Omit the batter to make a gluten-free dish.

Mixed Vegetable Yellow Curry

You don't often see sweet potatoes in curries, but I like how its sweetness contrasts with the spicy flavors. This yellow curry is popular in Singapore, Indonesia and Vietnam. You can add a cornucopia of other vegetables — broccoli, potatoes, green beans, etc. Just pay attention to cooking time and cut them in large pieces so they don't fall apart in the curry. My one rule for making curries: always make a large quantity, because it tastes better as leftovers!

PREP TIME: 20 MINUTES
COOK TIME: 35 MINUTES (10 MINUTES ACTIVE)
MAKES: 6 TO 8 SERVINGS

2 tablespoons vegetable oil

1½ cups (360 g) chopped yellow onion

2¼ teaspoons fine sea salt, divided

2 tablespoons Yellow Curry Powder (page 31)
  or store-bought Madras curry powder

4 to 6 dried hot red chilies, shoulders snipped and
  seeded as desired

2½ lbs (1.2 kg) orange sweet potatoes, peeled and
  cut into 2-in (5-cm) chunks

4 large carrots, peeled and chopped into
  2-in (5-cm) rounds

8 oz (500 g) cauliflower florets

One 14-oz (400-ml) can unsweetened coconut milk

1½ to 2 cups (325 to 500 ml) low-sodium vegetable
  stock or water

1 plump stalk lemongrass, trimmed and bruised

3 Asian (kaffir) lime leaves (optional)

6 hard-boiled eggs (optional)

Heat the oil in a large heavy pot or Dutch oven over medium heat until shimmering hot. Fry the onion until soft, 2 to 3 minutes. Add ¼ teaspoon of the salt, the Yellow Curry Powder and the dried chilies; stir until aromatic, 15 to 30 seconds. Add the sweet potatoes, carrots and cauliflower, and stir until well coated.

Pour in the coconut milk and 1½ cups (400 ml) of the vegetable stock or water, adding more if necessary to cover the vegetables. Add the lemongrass and lime leaves, if using. Bring to a boil over high heat, then lower the heat to a gentle simmer. Cover and cook for 10 minutes. Tuck the hard-boiled eggs, if using, into the sauce, turning occasionally so they color evenly. Simmer for another 15 to 20 minutes, until the sweet potatoes are tender and the gravy is thick. Stir in the remaining salt. Taste and adjust seasonings if necessary.

If possible, allow the curry to sit for at least 1 hour before serving for the vegetables to absorb the flavors. Before serving, remove the lemongrass and lime leaves. Serve hot with steamed jasmine rice or baguette slices.

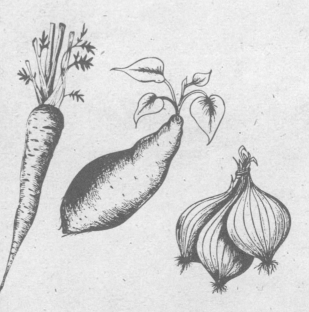

Adobo Ratatouille

I first discovered the concept of a vegetarian adobo in *The Adobo Road Cookbook* by Marvin Gapultos. In his recipe, Marvin uses myriad bell peppers for a colorful combo. As I read the recipe, it occurred to me that Filipino adobo and some French ratatouille recipes had a few things in common: both require simmering on the stovetop and the use of vinegar. I came up with a Franco-Filipino concoction that's a delightful cross-pollination of the two recipes.

PREP TIME: 15 MINUTES +
  30 MINUTES FOR SALTING
COOK TIME: 30 MINUTES
MAKES: 4 SERVINGS

Tip Traditional Filipino adobo uses either cane or coconut vinegar. Both are mild vinegars. If you only have a sharper type, such as sherry or red wine vinegar, use a little less and/or add more sugar.

1 baby globe eggplant (aubergine) (¾ lb/375 g)
1 medium zucchini (¾ lb/375 g)
1 teaspoon fine sea salt
4 tablespoons vegetable oil, divided
½ cup (75 g) sliced sweet onion
1 large red bell pepper, cut into strips
4 cloves garlic, smashed and peeled
2 large firm, ripe tomatoes, cut into 4 wedges each
¼ cup (60 ml) cane, apple cider, or other mild vinegar
¼ cup (60 ml) soy sauce
2 tablespoons dark brown sugar
1 teaspoon freshly ground black pepper
1 large bay leaf

Cut the eggplant and zucchini into strips about 3 inches (7.5 cm) long and 1 inch (2.5 cm) wide. Place in a colander and toss with the salt. Let stand for 30 minutes, then rinse and pat dry with paper towels.

Heat 2 tablespoons of the oil in a large, heavy pot or Dutch oven over medium-high heat. Arrange the eggplant and zucchini strips in one layer and brown for 1 minute on each side. Transfer to a plate and set aside.

Add the remaining 2 tablespoons of oil to the same pot over medium-high heat. Add the onions and peppers and cook, stirring, for 3 to 5 minutes, until the onions are translucent and the peppers start to wilt. Stir in the garlic and tomatoes. Reduce the heat to low and cook until the tomatoes render their juices, another 4 to 6 minutes.

Return the eggplant and zucchini to the pot and add the vinegar, soy sauce, brown sugar, pepper, and bay leaf. Stir to mix. Bring to a boil over high heat, then reduce the heat so that the mixture is bubbling gently. Cover and simmer for 10 minutes.

Uncover and simmer for another 10 minutes until the vegetables are tender and the liquid has thickened and reduced to about ½ cup. Stir occasionally to prevent the vegetables from scorching at the bottom of pot. Taste and add more seasonings as needed, or add water a little at a time if it's too vinegary. Remove the bay leaf and transfer to a serving dish. Serve with steamed jasmine rice.

Stuffed Cabbage Parcels

Stuffed vegetables are common in Chinese cuisine. Everything from eggplant to bitter melon can be stuffed, usually with fish or meat paste. This Indonesian-Chinese version is stuffed with tofu and served with peanut sauce. If you prefer making dainty parcels, choose a small head of cabbage and use 1 heaping tablespoon of filling per parcel; this will yield 16 parcels.

PREP TIME: 30 MINUTES
COOK TIME: 10 MINUTES
MAKES: 4 SERVINGS (8 PARCELS)

One 14 to 16-oz (400 to 500-g)
    package firm tofu
1 large shallot
2 cloves garlic, peeled
1 teaspoon finely chopped green
    onion (scallion), green parts only
1 teaspoon fine sea salt
¼ teaspoon freshly ground black
    pepper
1 egg, beaten (omit for a vegan
    dish)
1 medium head cabbage
1 large stalk green onion (scallion)
    or kitchen twine for tying the
    parcels
Fried Shallots (page 26), for
    garnish
Easy Peanut Sauce (page 38), for
    serving

Wrap the tofu in a non-terry kitchen towel and squeeze out as much liquid as possible. Transfer to a medium bowl and mash.

Blitz the shallot and garlic in a small food processor until reduced to confetti bits. Add to the tofu, along with the green onions, salt and pepper. Mix well, then taste and adjust seasonings if needed. Add the egg and stir to blend. This should make about 1½ cups of filling.

Cut the stem of the cabbage to release the leaves. Gently pry the leaves off without breaking them. Pull off 10 leaves (the extras are for patching).

Bring a large pot of salted water to a boil. Plunge the cabbage leaves in and cook for 1 minute or until they turn bright green and become pliable. Remove from the water and lay them on kitchen towels. Pat dry with another kitchen towel. Next, blanch the green onion stalk (if using) for 30 seconds, or until pliable.

When the vegetables are cool enough to handle, cut the green onion stalk lengthwise into eight "ribbons" for tying the parcels.

Lay out one cabbage leaf on a cutting board and spoon 2½ tablespoons of filling in the middle. Fold the leaf over the filling into a snug parcel and tie, seam-side down, with the green onion ribbons or kitchen twine. If the leaf breaks or you find holes, use the extra leaves as patches. Arrange the parcels in a steamer basket at least ½ in (1.5 cm) apart, working in batches if necessary.

Steam parcels until the filling is firm and the cabbage leaves turn dull green, 8 to 10 minutes.

Sprinkle with Fried Shallots and serve with Easy Peanut Sauce.

Red and Golden Beets in Green Curry

The combination of red and golden beets makes for a stunning dish. But you can use one or the other, depending on what's available at your grocery store or farmers' market. Look for beets that are firm and free of blemishes, with sturdy green leaves and stems that aren't floppy.

PREP TIME: 10 MINUTES

COOK TIME: 1 HOUR

MAKES: 4 SERVINGS

1½ lbs (750 g) red and golden beets, greens attached

2 tablespoons vegetable oil

1½ tablespoons prepared green curry paste, or to taste

2 fresh Thai or Serrano chilies, stemmed and seeded as desired (optional depending on the spiciness of your curry paste)

½ teaspoon fine sea salt

1 teaspoon coconut palm sugar or ¾ teaspoon dark brown sugar

1 teaspoon Vegan "Fish" Sauce (page 35) or soy sauce

1 cup (250 ml) water

¼ cup (10 g) Thai or Italian basil leaves

Tip For convenience, I like to buy Thai Kitchen brand curry pastes at my local grocery store. However, Asian markets will have a wider variety of brands to choose from. See page 19 for more information.

Cut or twist the greens from the beetroots. Rinse the greens under cold running water and drain briefly. Stack on the cutting board and slice into thin (¼-in/5-mm) ribbons, including the stalks. Set aside.

Trim and discard both ends of each beet bulb. Peel with a vegetable peeler and rinse under running water. Cut the bulbs into 1-inch (2.5-cm) cubes.

Swirl the oil into a large saucepan or small Dutch oven and set over medium-high heat. When shimmering hot, add the curry paste and cook, stirring, until aromatic, about 2 minutes. Add the beets and chilies (if using), stirring to coat with the paste. Reduce the heat to medium-low and cover. Cook for 10 to 15 minutes, stirring occasionally, until the beets are braising in their own juices.

Add the beet greens, salt, sugar, Vegan "Fish" Sauce and water, and raise the heat to medium-high. Once the curry comes to a boil, reduce the heat to a gentle simmer and cover. Cook, stirring occasionally, until the beets are tender and the liquid is reduced by about half, about 45 minutes. If you'd like a drier curry, uncover and raise the heat to medium-high to reduce the sauce as desired. Taste and adjust seasonings as needed. Remove from heat, add the basil and stir to mix. Serve with steamed jasmine rice.

Cherry Tomatoes Simmered with Tofu

Tomatoes simmered with tofu is a very common home-style Vietnamese dish. While it's quite bland on its own, tofu— especially fried tofu— absorbs flavors like a sponge. Fried tofu is also well suited for this simmering technique, because it retains its shape and won't fall apart.

PREP TIME: 10 MINUTES
COOK TIME: 10 MINUTES
MAKES: 4 SERVINGS

12 oz (350 g) Fried Golden Tofu (page 43) or
   store-bought fried tofu, cut into 1 x 2-in
   (2.5 x 5-cm) pieces
1 tablespoon vegetable oil
2 lbs (1 kg) red and yellow cherry or grape
   tomatoes, halved
¼ cup (60 ml) Vegan "Fish" Sauce (page 35)
2 tablespoons granulated sugar
¼ cup (25 g) chopped green onion (scallion),
   green parts only

Coat the bottom of a medium nonstick or cast-iron skillet with the oil. Arrange the tofu in a single layer. Wedge in the tomatoes wherever you can around the tofu. Pile the tomatoes on top of the tofu to form a second layer if you have to.

   Combine the Vegan "Fish" Sauce and sugar in a small bowl and stir to blend. Pour over the tofu and tomatoes in the skillet and scatter the green onions on top. Cover and simmer over medium heat until the tomatoes soften and release their juices, and their skins start to peel, 10 to 15 minutes. Serve hot with steamed jasmine rice.

General Tso's Eggplant

General Tso's Chicken is a staple at Chinese restaurants in the U.S.—everyone loves the crispy fried chicken tossed in tangy-sweet sauce. So I started hunting for a vegetable that could benefit from a similar preparation. My answer came along in the form of the shiny purple eggplant. (Hint: cauliflower comes in a close second.)

PREP TIME: 15 MINUTES + 30 MINUTES FOR SALTING
COOK TIME: 25 MINUTES
MAKES: 4 SERVINGS

1 baby globe or Italian eggplant (aubergine) (¾ lb/375 g), cut into 2 x 1-in (5 x 2.5-cm) pieces
1 teaspoon fine sea salt

Sauce

2 tablespoons sugar
1 teaspoon tomato paste
1 teaspoon potato starch or cornstarch
1½ tablespoons rice vinegar
1 tablespoon soy sauce
2 teaspoons sesame oil
¼ cup (60 ml) low-sodium vegetable stock or water

Batter

½ cup (60 g) all-purpose flour
½ cup (75 g) potato starch or cornstarch
1 tablespoon soy sauce
1 tablespoon Chinese cooking wine or dry sherry
Water and ice cubes

Vegetable oil for frying, plus 2 tablespoons for sauce
8 dried red chilies, shoulders snipped and seeds removed as desired
2 teaspoons finely chopped fresh ginger
2 teaspoons minced garlic
1 green onion (scallion), chopped, for garnish

Place the cut eggplant in a colander over the sink and sprinkle with the salt. Let sit for 30 minutes. Rinse and pat very dry.

Stir together the sugar, tomato paste, potato starch, rice vinegar, soy sauce, sesame oil, and stock or water in a small bowl until smooth to make the sauce. Set aside.

When you're ready to start frying, stir the flour and potato starch together in a large mixing bowl. Set aside ¼ cup (35 g) for dusting. Pour the soy sauce and cooking wine into a liquid measure. Fill with ice to about ½ cup (125 ml) and top off with water to ⅔ cup (165 ml). Stir, then pour into the flour bowl, mixing rapidly with chopsticks or a fork until just combined, no more than 30 seconds. The batter should be thin and lumpy, with the consistency of heavy cream. A few lumps here and there are fine, and any floating ice cubes will help keep the batter cool.

Pour enough oil into a wok or Dutch oven to reach a depth of 2 in (5 cm) and set over high heat until the oil reaches about 350°F (180°C) on a deep-fry thermometer. (See page 14 for more about deep frying.) Reduce the heat to medium to maintain temperature, and line a large plate with paper towels.

Dust the eggplant pieces in the reserved flour-potato-starch mix, shaking to remove excess. Dip them into the batter and fry in batches for 3 to 4 minutes, until crisp and golden. Don't overcrowd the wok. Remove with a slotted spoon and drain on paper towels. Keep warm in a 200°F (100°C) oven. Repeat until all the eggplant is cooked. Let the oil cool down a little and pour into a glass jar or other heatproof container, and set aside for another use. Wipe the wok clean.

Set the wok back on the stove over high heat. Swirl in the 2 tablespoons oil and heat until shimmering hot. Toss in the chilies and stir for a few seconds, until they just start to darken. Reduce the heat to medium and cook the ginger and garlic until aromatic, about 30 seconds. Pour in the sauce, stirring as it thickens. Return the eggplant to the wok and stir continuously to coat. Transfer to a serving platter and scatter with the green onions. Serve with steamed jasmine rice.

> **Tips** I've used a batter similar to that for Japanese tempura to give the eggplant a crisp, crunchy exterior. The same batter can be used to make vegetable tempura; eat it with Spicy Soy Dipping Sauce (page 37).
> • If you have time, lay the salted eggplant out to dry on paper towels for 30 minutes before dusting and frying.

Sweet Potato Rice Stew

Just about every Asian culture has a comforting rice stew that is a soothing remedy for a sick child (or even an adult). Compared to Chinese congee, this Thai-style rice stew is thinner and contains whole rice grains. However, as the stew sits, the rice grains continue to absorb water and the texture thickens. Like fried rice, this is a great way to use up leftover rice.

PREP TIME: 10 MINUTES
COOK TIME: 15 MINUTES
MAKES: 4 SERVINGS

1½ cups (250 g) peeled and cubed sweet potatoes (½ to ¾-in/1 to 2-cm cubes)

3½ cups (875 ml) low-sodium vegetable stock

2 cups (500 ml) water, plus more as needed

3 cups (450 g) cooked jasmine or other medium- to long-grain rice

1 tablespoon vegetable oil

3 tablespoons chopped garlic

2 tablespoons peeled and minced fresh ginger

1½ teaspoons fine sea salt, or to taste

1 tablespoon soy sauce

2 cups (250 g) spinach, arugula (rocket) or watercress

Garnishes
Sesame oil
Fried Shallots (page 26)
2 green onions, (scallions), green and white parts, chopped
Freshly ground black pepper

Combine the sweet potatoes, vegetable stock and water in a large pot over medium-high heat and bring to a gentle boil. Continue to cook until the sweet potatoes are just shy of tender, 2 to 3 minutes. Add the cooked rice and reduce the heat to a gentle simmer.

Heat the oil in a small nonstick or cast iron skillet over medium heat. Fry the garlic and ginger until golden and aromatic, 3 to 4 minutes. Reserve half the fried garlic and ginger for garnish and add the rest to the stew.

Simmer the stew for another 1 to 2 minutes, until the sweet potatoes are cooked to your liking and the rice grains are soft but still whole. The final dish should comprise about one-third soup and two-thirds rice grains. Simmer longer to reduce or add more water as needed.

Stir in the salt, soy sauce and greens, and remove from the heat. Ladle the rice stew into individual bowls. Drizzle with sesame oil and garnish with the reserved garlic and ginger, Fried Shallots, green onions and a grind or two of black pepper.

Stir-Fried Cellophane Noodles

Pancit, the universal Filipino crowd-pleaser, is usually made with egg noodles or rice noodles. This version, pancit sotanghon, uses bean thread noodles, commonly known as cellophane noodles or glass noodles. Cellophane noodles sometimes end up being too bland or too chewy, but I've circumvented this by soaking the noodles in vegetable stock first to both soften them and amp up their flavor. Enlivened by the tang of lemons, this dish is sure to be a hit at your next potluck or party.

PREP TIME: 20 MINUTES + 20 MINUTES
  SOAKING TIME
COOK TIME: 20 MINUTES
MAKES: 4 TO 6 SERVINGS

4 cups (1 liter) low-sodium vegetable stock

One 8-oz (250-g) package cellophane
  noodles (bean thread noodles)

2 tablespoons vegetable oil

2 tablespoons minced garlic

1 cup (150 g) sliced yellow onion

2 cups (200 g) chopped broccoli (cut to a
  similar size as the other vegetables)

4 cups (400 g) shredded cabbage

2 teaspoons fine sea salt, divided

2 large carrots with their green tops,
  peeled and cut into matchsticks (remove
  tops and reserve)

1 large red bell pepper, sliced

2 stalks celery, chopped

½ teaspoon freshly ground black pepper

1 teaspoon granulated sugar

3 green onions (scallions), cut into 1-in
  (2.5-cm) pieces

¼ cup (60 ml) soy sauce

3 tablespoons freshly squeezed lemon
  juice, plus lemon wedges for serving

Washed, chopped carrot tops for garnish

Chili paste such as sambal oelek

Bring the vegetable stock to a boil over high heat in a medium pot. Remove from the stove and add the cellophane noodles in batches, allowing the noodles to soften before adding more to the pot. Let the noodles soak until they are soft and the stock has been absorbed, about 20 minutes.

Swirl the oil into a large wok or skillet and set over high heat until shimmering hot. Fry the garlic and onions until aromatic and the onions turn translucent, about 1 minute. Add the broccoli, followed by the cabbage and 1 teaspoon of the salt. Next, add the carrots, then the bell pepper, then the celery, stirring for about 30 seconds between each addition.

Add the remaining 1 teaspoon salt, black pepper and sugar. Keep stirring and cooking until the vegetables are cooked to your liking, 3 to 4 minutes more.

Fluff the noodles to loosen the strands and toss them into the wok with the green onions. Stir to combine, then add the soy sauce and lemon juice and stir to coat. Taste and adjust seasonings as needed. When the noodles are heated through, dish onto a large serving platter. Garnish with the reserved carrot tops; serve with lemon wedges and chili paste in small dishes on the side.

Tips Pancit is a potluck favorite for many reasons: It's an easy dish to make to feed a crowd, and it can be made a day ahead and reheated on the stove before serving. Plus it's just as tasty served at room temperature.
  • If you have some on hand, sprinkle fried shallots and fried garlic over the noodles before serving.
  • Although it's not traditional, feel free to throw in tofu, mushrooms or egg to make this dish more substantial.

Vegetable and Egg Donburi Rice Bowl

This recipe is a vegetable-focused take on one of my favorite Japanese dishes, *oyako donburi* (chicken and egg over rice). It's easy to make for a simple solo meal and can be multiplied to feed a family. I often select my vegetables for their aesthetic value (I especially like delicata squash cut into pretty half-moons), but feel free to use whatever you can find.

PREP TIME: 10 MINUTES
COOK TIME: 6 MINUTES
MAKES: 1 SERVING

- ½ cup (125 ml) Dashi Seaweed Stock (page 29) or low-sodium vegetable stock
- 2 teaspoons soy sauce
- 1 teaspoon mirin
- 1 teaspoon granulated sugar
- ¼ cup (40 g) winter squash, such as delicata or kabocha, cut into bite-sized pieces
- 2 medium fresh shiitake mushrooms, stemmed and halved
- ⅛ cup (20 g) carrot cut into coins
- 5 snow peas or green beans
- 1 green onion (scallion), trimmed, white and green parts cut into 1-in (2.5-cm) lengths (reserve some for garnish)
- 1 large egg
- 1 cup (150 g) hot cooked rice

Tip If preferred, multiply the ingredients by the number of servings (no more than 4) and cook all at once in a single saucepan, then divide among the desired number of bowls of rice. Cooking times may be longer than stated above.

In a small (1 quart/liter) saucepan, combine the stock, soy sauce, mirin and sugar and bring to a gentle boil over medium-high heat.

Add the squash and mushrooms and simmer until the squash can be pierced with a fork but isn't fully cooked, about 4 minutes. Add the carrots and cook for about 2 minutes, then add the snow peas. (If you use a larger saucepan, you may need more liquid to cover the ingredients, but add sparingly).

While the vegetables are cooking, crack the egg into a small bowl and stir with chopsticks or a fork until well mixed but not foamy. When the vegetables are done to your liking, another 1 to 2 minutes, toss in the green onion. Then slowly pour in the egg, using a pair of chopsticks or a fork to slow down the flow, covering the entire surface of the pan. Don't stir. Cover and cook until egg is just set, about 30 to 45 seconds. The egg will be like a wet omelet. You can cook it longer if you like, but I recommend no more than 1 minute.

Scoop the rice into an oversized bowl. Ladle the vegetable and egg mixture over the rice, along with the desired amount of sauce. Garnish with the reserved green onions and serve immediately. Repeat for multiple servings.

Ice-Cold Korean Buckwheat Noodles

Cold noodles are common in many Asian cultures. *Naengmyeon* (literally "cold noodles") is the Korean version. The Korean buckwheat noodles used in this dish are chewier than the Japanese variety; they are often made with a combination of buckwheat and sweet potato or potato starch. This recipe is my version of *mul-naengmyon* ("water cold noodles"). It's especially refreshing when it's hot outside, or on that surprise Indian summer day in late September.

PREP TIME: 10 MINUTES
COOK TIME: 3 MINUTES
MAKES: 4 SERVINGS

One 12-oz (350-g) package of
   dried Korean buckwheat noodles
   (*naengmyeon*)
6 cups (1.5 liters) cold Dashi Seaweed
   Stock (page 29)
2 tablespoons plus 2 teaspoons rice
   vinegar
2 tablespoons plus 2 teaspoons
   granulated sugar
4 teaspoons fine sea salt
Ice cubes
2 Bosc pears or Fuji apples, peeled and
   sliced into thin wedges, submerged in
   salt water to prevent browning
½ cup (75 g) Homemade Spicy Kimchi
   (page 39) or Quick Vinegar Daikon
   and Carrot Pickles (preferably with
   cucumber substituted for carrot,
   page 40)
Homemade Korean Hot Pepper Paste
   (page 34) or Spicy Miso Dip (page 120)
4 large hard-cooked eggs, halved
Sesame oil, for garnish
Toasted sesame seeds, for garnish

Bring a large pot of water to a rolling boil over high heat. Add the dried noodles to the pot in a circular motion, separating the noodles around the pot. Cook until al dente, 3 to 5 minutes, stirring occasionally so they don't stick. Don't overcook them or they'll be gummy! Drain the noodles into a colander and rinse under cold running water several times to remove excess starch. Drain again and set aside until ready to serve.

In a large pot or bowl, combine the Dashi Seaweed Stock, rice vinegar, sugar and salt. Stir vigorously until the salt and sugar have completely dissolved. Taste and adjust seasonings as needed to achieve a good balance of sweet, salty and sour.

To serve, divide the noodles among 4 large bowls. Pour 1½ cups (375 ml) of broth into each bowl. Add 3 to 4 ice cubes to each bowl. Arrange pear slices, kimchi or pickles, Korean red pepper paste, and 2 egg halves on top of each serving. Drizzle with sesame oil and sprinkle with sesame seeds. Serve with extra vinegar and soy sauce on the side.

Tip If you can't find Korean buckwheat noodles (the package will be labeled *naengmyeon*), *dangmyeon* (Korean sweet potato noodles used for making *japchae*) or even Japanese buckwheat noodles will do.

Mushu Vegetable "Burritos"

I've only ever seen mushu pork, a quintessential Chinese-American dish, at restaurants in the U.S. Not being familiar with it, I never ordered it. However, my American-born husband ordered it one day, despite my protestations that it wasn't real Chinese food. I had to eat my words, because it was very tasty; it's also fun to make. Now I make this dish using ready-made tortillas (choose the smallest, thinnest ones you can find) instead of making the Chinese pancakes from scratch. My son loves that he can make his own dinner and eat it with his fingers!

PREP TIME: 20 MINUTES (LESS IF USING READY CUT VEGETABLES)
COOK TIME: 15 MINUTES
MAKES: 4 TO 6 SERVINGS

Sauce

1 tablespoon soy sauce
1 tablespoon Chinese cooking wine or dry
  sherry (optional)
1 tablespoon water
1 teaspoon granulated sugar
1 teaspoon cornstarch
1 teaspoon sesame oil
¼ teaspoon fine sea salt

Filling

4 large eggs
¼ teaspoon fine sea salt
Dash of sesame oil
Freshly ground black pepper
3 tablespoons vegetable oil, divided
1 tablespoon minced garlic
1 tablespoon peeled and minced fresh
  ginger
4 oz (100 g) button mushrooms, sliced
4 cups (400 g) shredded cabbage
2 medium carrots, shredded
1 cup (100 g) bean sprouts
4 green onions, green parts cut into
  1½-in (4-cm) lengths, bottom 4 in (10 cm)
  reserved for Green Onion Brushes
  if desired (see sidebar)

Twelve 8-in (20-cm) wheat tortillas
12 leaves romaine or butter lettuce (optional)
Hoisin sauce, for serving
Chili paste like *sambal oelek*, for serving

Make the Sauce: Whisk together the soy sauce, cooking wine (if using), water, sugar, cornstarch, sesame oil, and salt in a small bowl. Set aside.

Make the Filling: In a medium-sized bowl, whisk together the eggs, salt, sesame oil and a grind of black pepper. Swirl 1 tablespoon of the oil into a large wok or skillet and set over medium heat until shimmering hot. Pour in the eggs and swirl to cover the entire cooking surface. Cook undisturbed until eggs start to set, 1 to 2 minutes. Break up into large curds and continue to cook, stirring, for 45 seconds to 1 minute. Slide onto a plate and set aside.

Wipe out the wok and heat the remaining 2 tablespoons of oil over medium-high heat. Fry the garlic and ginger until aromatic, about 30 seconds. Add the mushrooms; stir and cook for 1 minute. Add the cabbage; stir and cook for 4 to 5 minutes. Add the carrots; stir and cook for 1 to 2 minutes more, or until the vegetables are almost cooked to your liking. Add the bean sprouts and the sliced green onion tops. Whisk the Sauce again and add, stirring to coat the vegetables. Fold in the egg and continue to cook, stirring, until the egg is heated through and cooked to your liking. Scoop the Filling onto a serving platter. Serve with warm tortillas and lettuce leaves (if using), with the hoisin sauce and chili sauce in small dishes on the side.

To eat, lay a lettuce leaf, if using, on a tortilla. If desired, use a Green Onion Brush to paint hoisin sauce and chili paste on the lettuce. Scoop a tablespoon or two of the Filling onto the tortilla. Fold like a burrito, leaving one end open. Enjoy!

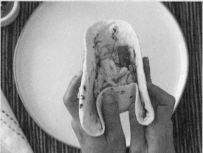

Tip To make a quick midweek dinner, buy ready-cut vegetables at the store: sliced mushrooms, shredded carrots and cabbage (look for cabbage packaged as Angel Hair or coleslaw cabbage).

Green Onion Brushes

Making these green onion brushes is optional, but they certainly add to the fun! Use a sharp knife or scissors to shred the ends of each green onion. Toss in a bowl of ice water for 30 minutes to let the shreds curl.

WINTER RECIPES

Winter vegetables can be hard to love. Unlike the rainbow-hued vegetables of spring and summer, winter's bounty is cloaked in shades of beige, green, darker green and the occasional orange.

As dull and unexciting these vegetables may seem, I've realized there is hope if you put on your culinary thinking cap. Just like winter's freezing temperatures and four-foot snow drifts, it's all about perspective.

Looking at winter vegetables in a different light can give meals new meaning and flavors. Brussels sprouts evolve from boiled *blech* to Roasted Brussels Sprouts with Sweet Chili Sauce. Panko breadcrumbs gussy up boring mashed root vegetables into Winter Squash Croquettes.

Creamy coconut milk and fiery chilies can transport any winter greens

Rainbow Chard Korean Pancake (page 124)

Peppery Turmeric Soup (page 126)

to the tropics, as in Winter Greens and Tofu in Spicy Coconut Sauce.

Over the years, I've learned to embrace the winters, cabbage recipes, snow storms, et al. Here are some of the things I enjoy most in the winter:

• Citrus fruit! Because of their sunny color and constitution, I was surprised to learn

STARTERS & SNACKS

Tofu, Spinach and
Fennel Wontons

Raw Vegetable Platter
with Spicy Miso Dip

Korean-Style Buffalo
Broccoli

Winter Squash
Croquettes

Rainbow Chard
Korean Pancake

FAMILY-STYLE DISHES

Peppery Turmeric Soup

Kung Pao Potatoes

Roasted Brussels Sprouts
with Sweet Chili Sauce

Sweet Soy and Black
Pepper Cauliflower

Burmese-Style Pumpkin and
Parsnip Curry

Winter Greens and Tofu
in Spicy Coconut Sauce

ALL-IN-ONE MEALS

Swiss Chard Brown Rice
Sushi Hand Rolls

White Curry Soup with
Pressed Rice Cakes

Warming Vegetable Pho

Easy Miso Ramen

Wintry Kimchi Stew

Red Curry Noodles with
Roasted Cauliflower and
Rainbow Carrots

that oranges, lemons and the like were harvested in the dead of winter—in warm places
like California and Florida, of course.

• Bitter greens—oh my, how I've learned to
love my bitter greens! Whether in Kale "Chips" or
Rainbow Chard Korean Pancake, bitter greens
have found a place in my heart.

• I call the muted, low-lying light that fills
my kitchen on winter afternoons the "golden
glow." Wrapped in its warm embrace, I feel
calm, peaceful and content.

Sadly, my farmers' market closes during winter. Instead, I rely on my local grocery store,
which thankfully carries local and seasonal
produce, to make the likes of Kung Pao Potatoes
(page 127) and Warming Vegetable Pho (page 136).

Kung Pao Potatoes (page 127)

Tofu, Spinach and Fennel Wontons

These dumplings have a very poetic name: "wonton" (*yun tun* in Mandarin) means "swallowing clouds." Indeed, your mouth will feel like it's wrapping itself around a cloud—in fact, a pillow filled with soft tofu and spinach combined with the slight crunch of fennel. If you don't like the anise taste in fennel, just cook it a little longer and the flavor will dissipate. You can also choose to boil the wontons in soup or deep-fry them!

PREP TIME: 30 MINUTES

COOK TIME: 20 MINUTES

MAKES: 4 TO 6 SERVINGS (24 WONTONS)

Filling

4 oz (120 g) extra-firm tofu

2 tablespoons vegetable oil

1 teaspoon grated fresh ginger

½ cup (60 g) diced fennel bulb

6 cups packed (120 g) baby spinach or spinach leaves, coarsely chopped

⅛ teaspoon fine sea salt

Freshly ground black pepper

¼ teaspoon granulated sugar

1 teaspoon soy sauce

1 teaspoon sesame oil

1 tablespoon chopped green onion (scallion), green parts only

½ teaspoon chopped fennel fronds

24 square wonton wrappers (plus a few extras in case of tears)

Spicy Wonton Dipping Sauce (see sidebar)

Make the Filling: place the tofu in a non-terry kitchen towel and wring out as much liquid as possible. You'll have about ⅔ cup crumbled tofu.

Swirl the vegetable oil into a large wok or skillet and set over medium heat. When shimmering hot, add the ginger and fry until aromatic, about 30 seconds. Add the chopped fennel and cook, stirring, for about 1 minute until translucent. Add the spinach; continue to stir and cook for about 1 minute until wilted. Add the tofu, salt, a grind of black pepper, sugar, soy sauce, and sesame oil and mix well until heated through. Taste and adjust seasonings as needed.

Turn off the heat and stir in the green onions and fennel fronds. Transfer to a bowl and set aside to cool completely. You should have about 1½ cups of filling. (Filling can be prepared 1 day in advance and refrigerated; bring to room temperature before assembling the wontons.)

To assemble the wontons, set up your work station: Fill a small bowl with water; prepare a kitchen towel for wiping your fingers; have your filling ready; line a steamer basket with parchment paper; and cover the stack of wonton wrappers with a damp towel.

Hold a wrapper in your left (or non-dominant) hand. Place ½ tablespoon filling in the middle, pressing and shaping it into a flat mound and leaving a ½- to ¾-inch (1.5- to 2-cm) border on all sides. Gently moisten the edges of the wrapper with your other finger.

Fold one corner of the wonton wrapper over the filling to meet the opposite corner to form a triangle. Seal the edges, carefully pushing out air. Pull the two bottom corners of the triangle together and cross them in a "hug."

> **Tips** My recipe tester Niki Stojnic sets up a wonton assembly line for efficient folding. She puts four wonton wrappers on her work surface, moistens the edges of all four, places filling in each, then folds them in turn, first making triangles, then crossing the "arms" and moistening to seal. Niki also deep-fried some of the wontons.
>
> • To freeze, leave the wontons on the baking sheet and freeze until hard (about 1 hour), then tip them into a zip-top freezer bag, pressing out excess air before sealing. Frozen wontons will keep for 1 to 2 months. To cook, thaw completely on a parchment-lined steamer tray. Use your finger to smooth over any cracks before steaming.

Moisten the corners with a little water and pinch to seal. If steaming right away, place the finished dumpling on the steamer basket, sealed side up. If not, place the wontons ½ inch (1.5 cm) apart on a parchment-lined baking sheet that has been dusted with flour.

Repeat, keeping the finished wontons covered with a dry kitchen towel as you work. (Assembled wontons can be covered with plastic wrap and refrigerated for several hours. Cook them straight from the refrigerator.)

Steam the wontons over boiling water for about 8 minutes, or until the wrappers are slightly puffed and translucent. (See page 14 for steaming tips.) Remove the basket and transfer the wontons to a plate.

Serve immediately with the Spicy Wonton Dipping Sauce, either in a communal bowl with a spoon or portioned into individual bowls.

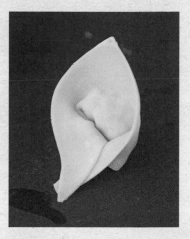

Spicy Wonton Dipping Sauce

PREP TIME: 10 MINUTES + 5 MINUTES COOLING TIME
MAKES: ½ CUP

2 to 4 dried red chilies, shoulders snipped and seeds shaken out
1 teaspoon Sichuan peppercorns or ½ teaspoon Tellicherry black peppercorns
1 tablespoon sesame seeds
3 tablespoons vegetable oil
1 tablespoon sesame oil
1 tablespoon rice vinegar
1 tablespoon Chinese black vinegar or balsamic vinegar
1 tablespoon soy sauce
2 teaspoons granulated sugar
1 tablespoon minced garlic

Toast the chilies, peppercorns and sesame seeds in a dry skillet over medium heat until aromatic and lightly browned, 2 to 3 minutes. Transfer to a mortar and grind with a pestle until the chilies resemble crushed red pepper flakes, the peppercorns are a coarse powder, and most of the sesame seeds are crushed (leave about a quarter whole). Transfer to a heatproof bowl.

Heat the vegetable oil in a small skillet over medium heat until shimmering hot. Immediately pour over the chili-peppercorn mixture. After the sizzling dies down, let cool for 5 minutes.

Combine the sesame oil, rice vinegar, Chinese black vinegar, soy sauce, sugar and garlic in a medium bowl and whisk until the sugar completely dissolves. Add the chili oil mixture, stir and set aside until ready to use.

Tip The sauce can be made ahead and refrigerated in a sealed container for 3 to 4 days.

Raw Vegetable Platter with Spicy Miso Dip

Several years ago, I was helping my friend Deb Samuels (author of *My Japanese Table*) with her bento-making workshop organized by the Smithsonian Associates in Washington, D.C. One of the items on the menu was a spicy dip served with an assortment of cut vegetables. Lucky me, I went home with a full jar of the dip at the end of the night! Later, I realized it was *ssamjang*, the Korean condiment used to spice up grilled meats wrapped in lettuce. I soon discovered that ssamjang has myriad uses. You can mix it with mayo to slather on burgers and use as a condiment for sushi hand rolls, use it to make a ramen soup base, or use it to accompany any food that pairs with mayo or chili paste.

PREP TIME: 30 MINUTES
MAKES: 8 TO 10 SERVINGS

5 to 6 cups (1 kg) of the following vegetables:
  Radicchio cut into wedges
  Carrots cut into sticks
  Cucumbers cut into spears
  Fennel cut into petals
  Radishes cut into rounds

Spicy Miso Dip

½ cup (125 g) red or white miso
3 tablespoons Homemade Korean Hot Pepper Paste (page 34) or chili paste like *sambal oelek*
2 tablespoons toasted sesame seeds, crushed
2 teaspoons minced garlic
5 tablespoons water
2 tablespoons honey
2 tablespoons sesame oil

Arrange the cut vegetables on a large platter.
  Whisk together the miso, Homemade Korean Hot Pepper Paste, sesame seeds, garlic, water, honey, and sesame oil in a large bowl until smooth. Spoon into a pretty bowl and serve with the vegetables.

Tip Stored in an airtight container, the dip will keep in the refrigerator for up to 3 months.

Korean-Style Buffalo Broccoli

For this veggie mashup of Korean fried chicken wings and everyone's favorite bar food, buffalo wings, I've coated broccoli florets in tempura batter to produce a crispy, lacy layer. The broccoli is then tossed in a sweet and spicy sauce for an appetizer that can't be beat.

PREP TIME: 20 MINUTES
COOK TIME: 25 MINUTES
MAKES: 4 TO 6 SERVINGS

2 lbs (1 kg) broccoli (2 medium crowns)

Sauce
1 tablespoon minced garlic
1 tablespoon minced fresh ginger
¼ cup (60 g) Homemade Korean Hot Pepper Paste (page 34)
¼ cup (60 ml) soy sauce
1 tablespoon sesame oil
1 tablespoon rice vinegar
1 tablespoon honey
½ teaspoon freshly ground black pepper

Batter
1 cup (120 g) all-purpose flour
1 cup (115 g) cornstarch
Fine sea salt and freshly ground pepper to taste (optional)
1⅓ cups (335 ml) cold water with ice
Vegetable oil, for frying

Garnishes
1 tablespoon chopped green onion (scallion), green and white parts
1 tablespoon toasted sesame seeds
2 to 3 dried red chilies, stemmed, seeded as desired and chopped

Trim the broccoli and cut into bite-sized florets. Save the stems for another use. You'll have about 4 cups.

To make the Sauce, whisk together the garlic, ginger, Homemade Korean Hot Pepper Paste, soy sauce, sesame oil, rice vinegar, honey, and black pepper in a large bowl until smooth.

When you are ready to start frying, make the Batter. Combine the flour and cornstarch in a large mixing bowl. Remove ½ cup (60 g), season with salt and pepper, if using, and set aside on a rimmed plate for dusting. Pour the ice water into the bowl with the flour and cornstarch, mixing rapidly with chopsticks or a fork until just combined, no more than 30 seconds. The Batter should be thin and lumpy with the consistency of heavy cream. A few lumps here and there are fine, and any floating ice cubes will help keep the batter cool.

Make sure the florets are completely dry (towel them dry if necessary). Dust them with the reserved flour-cornstarch mixture to coat lightly.

Pour enough oil into a medium heavy pot or Dutch oven to reach a depth of 2 in (5 cm) and set over high heat until it reaches 350°F (180°C) on a deep-fry thermometer (see page 14 for more deep-frying tips). Once it has reached the right temperature, reduce the heat to medium. Set up a rack on a baking sheet or line it with paper towels.

Working with a few florets at a time, shake off excess flour-cornstarch mixture and dip in the batter. Let excess batter drip off. Frying in batches, slip the florets into the oil and cook for about 30 seconds, gently spooning oil over them. Roll the florets in the oil for another 30 to 45 seconds until golden and crispy all over. Remove them with a slotted spoon and drain on paper towels. Keep warm in a 200°F (100°C) oven. Bring the oil temperature back up to 350°F (180°C) and remove any debris in the oil. Repeat until all the florets are fried.

When ready to serve, toss the florets in the sauce. Sprinkle with green onions, sesame seeds and chopped dried chilies, and serve immediately.

Winter Squash Croquettes

Making croquettes is a fine way to use up leftover bits of squash and root vegetables. And if I have any cooked meats or vegetables lying around, I'll throw those into the mix as well. Personally, I like to combine a sweet item, like kabocha squash or parsnip, with potatoes to balance the flavor. But you can mix and match any way you want. Roasting deepens and sweetens the flavor of the squash and potatoes. However, you can also steam or simmer them. Peel and cut the vegetables into small chunks and cook for 10 to 15 minutes, until tender.

PREP TIME: 15 MINUTES + COOLING TIME
COOK TIME: 1 HOUR
MAKES: 4 SERVINGS (8 CROQUETTES)

8 oz (250 g) winter squash such as kabocha, delicata or kuri

8 oz (250 g) floury potatoes such as russet

1 teaspoon fine sea salt, divided

Freshly ground black pepper, to taste

2 tablespoons vegetable oil, plus more for frying

3 tablespoons cornstarch, divided

1 large egg, beaten

1 to 2 tablespoons milk

½ to ¾ cup (25 to 35 g) panko breadcrumbs

¼ cup (60 g) very finely chopped yellow onion

¼ cup (30 g) frozen peas, defrosted

Fine sea salt, to taste

> **Tips** For an easy dipping sauce, mix equal parts of ketchup and tonkatsu sauce—or simply drizzle with tonkatsu sauce.
>
> • To make this dish vegan, use soy milk instead of milk and omit the egg.
>
> • If you don't fancy the taste of raw onion, cook them first before adding to the mashed veggies: Swirl 2 teaspoons oil into a small skillet and set over medium heat until shimmering hot. Add the onions and cook, stirring, for 3 to 4 minutes until translucent and lightly brown on the edges.

Preheat oven to 400°F (205°C).

Remove the seeds from the squash and cut into 4 to 6 wedges. Cut the potatoes in half lengthwise.

Lay the squash and potatoes on a greased, foil-lined baking sheet. Season with ⅛ teaspoon of the salt and a grind of pepper. Drizzle with 1 to 2 tablespoons vegetable oil. Roast until tender, about 45 minutes, and set aside to cool.

When cool, scoop out the flesh and discard the skins. Mash coarsely with a potato masher or fork. You'll have about 1½ cups of mashed vegetables. Fold in the onions and peas. Season with ½ teaspoon salt and a grind of pepper. Taste and adjust seasonings as needed.

If you aren't in a hurry, or are making ahead, refrigerate the mixture to cool completely.

To assemble the croquettes, set up your work station: Place 2 tablespoons of the cornstarch in a small rimmed dish; mix the egg and milk together in a small bowl; place the panko in another dish; line a plate with parchment to hold the assembled croquettes.

Dust your hands with the remaining 1 tablespoon cornstarch and divide the mashed vegetables into 8 portions. Shape each portion into a log about 3 inches (7.5 cm) long and 1 inch (2.5 cm) in diameter (you can make them football- or golf ball-shaped if you like). Roll the logs in cornstarch and shake to remove excess. All surfaces should be lightly coated.

Dip a log into the egg mixture, then roll in the panko. Lightly press more panko to cover any gaps. Place the breaded croquette on the plate. Repeat until all the croquettes are breaded. You can do this several hours ahead, but cover them and refrigerate if you'll be waiting more than 30 minutes.

Pour enough vegetable oil into a large wok or Dutch oven to reach a depth of 1 in (2.5 cm) and set over medium high heat until it reaches 350°F (180°C). If you don't have a deep-fry ther-

How to Bake the Croquettes

Place the rack in the top third of the oven. Preheat to 400°F (205°C). Grease a rimmed baking sheet with 2 tablespoons vegetable oil and place it in the oven for 10 minutes. Remove. Brush the croquettes on all sides with oil and gently place them on the prepared sheet (careful—it will be hot). Bake the croquettes for 10 minutes, then roll them a quarter-turn and bake for 4 minutes. Turn and bake 2 more times, each time for 4 minutes, until crispy and golden all over.

mometer, toss in some panko breadcrumbs. If they sink, then float slowly to the top sizzling, your oil is ready.

Frying in batches, slip the croquettes into the oil and cook for about 1 minute, gently spooning oil over them. Flip and fry until golden all over, another 30 seconds to 1 minute.

Remove the croquettes with a slotted spoon and drain on paper towels. (I don't recommend using a rack as they are very soft.) Remove any debris and bring the oil back up to temperature. Repeat until all the croquettes are fried.

Sprinkle with sea salt and serve warm or at room temperature with sauce alongside (see Tips on opposite page).

Rainbow Chard Korean Pancake

In this hearty Korean staple, rice flour adds texture for crispy edges while leaving the middle slightly chewy. But even if you omit it, the pancakes will still be tasty. Aim for a consistency that's between crepe batter and American pancake batter. The batter should coat the back of a spoon and drip down in a thick stream. Admittedly, I've never been good at flipping pancakes and omelets, so I sometimes divide up the batter into smaller portions and make smaller pancakes.

PREP TIME: 15 MINUTES + COOLING TIME
COOK TIME: 30 MINUTES
MAKES: 4 SERVINGS (2 LARGE PANCAKES)

1¼ cups (150 g) all-purpose flour
⅓ cup (150 g) rice flour
1½ cups (375 ml) water
8 oz (250 g) rainbow chard
5 tablespoons vegetable oil, divided
½ cup (75 g) sliced yellow onion
Fine sea salt
Soy and Green Onion Dipping Sauce (see sidebar)

Mix the all-purpose and rice flours together with the water in a large mixing bowl.

Gently tear or cut the chard leaves from the center ribs. Chop the ribs into ½-in (1.5-cm) pieces. Stack the leaves and roll lengthwise into cigars, then cut crosswise into ½-in (1.5-cm) ribbons. Keep ribs and leaves separate. You'll have about 1 cup ribs and 3 cups packed leaves.

Swirl 1 tablespoon of the oil in a medium nonstick or cast-iron skillet and set over medium-high heat until shimmering hot. Add the onion and chard ribs. Cook, stirring, for about 2 minutes, until the onions turn translucent. Add the ribs and continue to stir and cook for another 2 to 3 minutes. Stir in the leaves and a pinch of salt, then cook until they wilt, another 2 to 3 minutes. Remove from the heat and allow to cool for about 5 minutes. Fold the chard and onions into the batter.

Wipe out the skillet and heat 1 tablespoon oil over medium-high heat for 30 seconds. Pour half the batter into the skillet, tilting and swirling so the batter forms an even layer. The pancake should be about ¼-in (0.5-cm) thick. Cook, shaking the skillet occasionally, until the bottom is golden brown, 3 to 4 minutes. Lift up one edge and pour in 1 more tablespoon oil, then flip the pancake carefully and press down with a spatula to flatten it and ensure it cooks thoroughly.

Cook until the pancake is golden brown on the bottom and the edges are crisp, another 1 to 2 minutes. Turn and press down on the pancake 2 to 3 more times until the pancake is cooked through.

Transfer the pancake to a serving platter and keep warm in a 200°F (100°C) oven. Repeat with the remaining batter.

To serve, cut each pancake into 8 slices and serve with Soy and Green Onion Dipping Sauce.

Soy and Green Onion Dipping Sauce

This sauce keeps for at least 3 days in the refrigerator, up to 1 week if you leave the green onions out until just before serving. Extra sauce? Dip fried tofu into it or toss with fresh greens.

MAKES: 1½ CUPS (375 ML)

¼ cup (60 ml) soy sauce
2 tablespoons rice vinegar
2 tablespoons water
1½ tablespoons sesame oil
1½ tablespoons honey
2 tablespoons roasted sesame seeds, crushed with a mortar and pestle
2 teaspoons coarse chili pepper flakes or chili paste
2 green onions (scallions), green and white parts, chopped

Whisk all ingredients together in a bowl and refrigerate until ready to serve.

Peppery Turmeric Soup

My mom used to slice potatoes into thin ovals and fry them into *kripik* (Indonesian for crisps or chips). But now she just buys bags of chips off the shelf. The brittle potato chips complement the tender potatoes, slippery cellophane noodles, firm bean sprouts and soft egg in the bowl.

PREP TIME: 15 MINUTES
COOK TIME: 20 MINUTES
MAKES: 4 SERVINGS

1 tablespoon vegetable oil
1 tablespoon minced garlic
1 teaspoon grated fresh ginger
1 tablespoon minced shallot
1 teaspoon ground turmeric powder
4½ cups (1.25 liters) low-sodium
   vegetable stock
1 plump stalk lemongrass, trimmed
   and smashed
2 Asian (kaffir) lime leaves (optional)
1½ teaspoons fine sea salt
½ teaspoon granulated sugar
¼ teaspoon freshly ground black pepper,
   or to taste
1 large yellow potato, peeled and cut
   into 1-in (2.5-cm) cubes
2 oz (50 g) cellophane noodles
2 large hard-boiled eggs, halved
   lengthwise
1 cup (100 g) bean sprouts or shredded
   cabbage, blanched
1 green onion (scallion), white and green
   parts, chopped
2 tablespoons Fried Shallots (page 26)
¼ cup (5 g) chopped celery leaves or
   flat-leaf parsley
½ cup (75 g) plain potato chips, crushed
1 large lime cut into wedges
Chili paste like *sambal oelek*
Sweet Soy Sauce (page 86)

Heat the oil in a large saucepan over medium-high heat until shimmering hot. Fry the garlic, ginger, and shallots until aromatic, 30 seconds to 1 minute. Stir in the turmeric powder and cook for another 30 seconds.

Pour in the stock and drop in the lemongrass and lime leaves, if using. Season with the salt, sugar and pepper. Add the potatoes and simmer until tender, 15 to 20 minutes. Taste and adjust seasonings as needed. Remove the lemongrass and lime leaves.

While the soup is simmering, soak the cellophane noodles in boiling water for 10 to 15 minutes or until soft. Drain and set aside.

To serve, divide the noodles, egg halves, and bean sprouts among 4 bowls. Pour ½ to ¾ cup soup into each bowl and garnish with green onions, Fried Shallots, celery leaves, and potato chips. Serve immediately with steamed jasmine rice and lime wedges, with the chili paste and Sweet Soy Sauce in small dishes alongside.

Tip For perfect hard-boiled eggs, place eggs in a saucepan large enough to hold them in a single layer. Cover with water by about 1 inch (2.5 cm). Bring to a boil over high heat then turn off the heat. Cover with a lid and let sit for 14 minutes. Drain the eggs and immerse in an ice bath until cool.

Kung Pao Potatoes

For these, I borrowed a tip from Kenji J. Lopez's breakfast hash recipe on SeriousEats.com: par-cooking the potatoes in vinegar-spiked water produces cubes that are firm on the outside yet fluffy on the inside. Plus, the potatoes don't fall apart during stir-frying. I prefer Yukon Gold potatoes— they're flavorful and withstand both dry and wet cooking methods. But any firm yellow potato will do.

PREP TIME: 15 MINUTES
COOK TIME: 15 MINUTES
MAKES: 4 SERVINGS

1 to 1¼ lbs (500 g) yellow potatoes (5 to 6 medium), peeled, cut into ¾-in (2-cm) cubes and submerged in cold water to prevent browning

2 tablespoons white distilled vinegar

1 tablespoon kosher salt or coarse sea salt

1 teaspoon potato starch or cornstarch

Sauce

1 tablespoon potato starch or cornstarch

1 tablespoon granulated sugar

½ teaspoon fine sea salt

1 tablespoon Chinese cooking wine or dry sherry

1 tablespoon Chinese black vinegar or balsamic vinegar

2 teaspoons soy sauce

1 teaspoon sesame oil

2 tablespoons water

2 tablespoons vegetable oil

4 to 8 dried red chilies, shoulders snipped and seeds shaken out as desired

1 teaspoon whole Sichuan peppercorns, crushed with a mortar and pestle

1 tablespoon minced garlic

1 tablespoon minced fresh ginger

2 green onions (scallions), chopped

½ cup (100 g) roasted peanuts

Place the potatoes in a large pot with 6 cups (1.5 liters) cold water. Add the distilled white vinegar and salt. Bring to a boil over high heat and then cook for 4 to 5 minutes more, until the potatoes are just shy of tender. Test a piece with a fork; the potato should give, but not fall apart. Drain, rinse with cold water and let sit in a colander to dry for 5 to 10 minutes. Transfer potato pieces to a bowl and toss with 1 teaspoon potato starch until well coated.

While the potatoes are cooking, make the Sauce. Whisk together the 1 tablespoon potato starch, the sugar, salt, cooking wine, black vinegar, soy sauce, sesame oil and water, and set aside.

Preheat a large wok or skillet. Swirl in the vegetable oil and set over high heat until shimmering hot. Add the chilies and Sichuan peppercorns and let them sizzle for about 30 seconds, until the chilies start to darken.

Add the cooked potatoes. Stir and cook until they start to brown, 3 to 4 minutes, then add the garlic and ginger. Cook, stirring, until aromatic, about 30 seconds.

Whisk the sauce again and pour it into the wok, stirring quickly as it thickens. Taste and adjust seasonings as needed. Throw in the green onions and peanuts; stir and cook for about 30 seconds until the green onions turn bright green. Remove from heat and serve immediately with steamed jasmine rice.

Roasted Brussels Sprouts with Sweet Chili Sauce

The ingredients in this dish are used to marinate Thai-style grilled chicken (*gai yang*). Instead of using sweet chili sauce for dipping, I toss the Brussels sprouts in it. Sweet chili sauce can be found in the international aisle of most grocery stores. It's perfect for dipping dumplings, egg rolls and adding to stir-fries. Making it at home is pretty simple, but if you'd rather buy a bottle, my favorite brand is Mae Ploy.

PREP TIME: 10 MINUTES
COOK TIME: 20 MINUTES
MAKES: 4 SERVINGS

2 tablespoons vegetable oil
1 tablespoon minced garlic
1 tablespoon minced shallot
1 lb (500 g) Brussels sprouts,
   trimmed and halved
½ teaspoon fine sea salt
¼ teaspoon freshly ground black pepper

Sauce
2 tablespoons Sweet Chili Sauce (page 37)
1 teaspoon Vegan "Fish" Sauce (page 35)
1 teaspoon warm water
½ cup (15 g) loosely packed coriander
   leaves (cilantro), finely chopped, divided

Tip To make on the stovetop, place the sprouts in a microwave-safe bowl with 1 inch of water. Cover and microwave for 3 minutes until bright green. Fry the garlic and shallot as directed above. Then arrange as many Brussels sprouts as space allows cut-side down in the skillet. Let them cook undisturbed until they start to brown, about 2 minutes. Season with salt and pepper, then stir and cook on high for 2 to 4 more minutes, until the ingredients are caramelized and tender. Toss with sauce and serve as directed.

Place a large, oven-safe skillet (cast iron works well) in the oven and preheat to 450°F (230°C).

Transfer the hot skillet to the stove and set over high heat. Add the oil, followed by the garlic and shallot. Fry until aromatic, 30 to 45 seconds. Next, add the Brussels sprouts and toss to combine. Season with salt and pepper and return the skillet to the oven. Roast for 15 to 20 minutes, until the ingredients are caramelized and tender, jiggling the pan halfway through so that the sprouts cook evenly.

While the sprouts are roasting, make the Sauce. Whisk together the Sweet Chili Sauce, Vegan "Fish" Sauce, warm water, and half of the coriander leaves in a large serving bowl.

When the Brussels sprouts are done, remove them from the oven and toss with the sauce to coat evenly. Transfer to a serving dish and garnish with the remaining coriander leaves. Serve immediately with steamed jasmine rice.

Sweet Soy and Black Pepper Cauliflower

In Yotam Ottolenghi's amazing vegetable cookbook *Plenty*, I discovered a recipe called "Black Pepper Tofu." According to the headnote, Ottolenghi learned to make the dish from a Singaporean friend. At first glance, the recipe looked totally unfamiliar, but the longer I stared at the ingredients, the more familiar it looked. Then I made it. It turns out that the ingredients and cooking method are very similar to one of Singapore's signature dishes, black pepper crab. I loved the flavors and wanted to adapt them to a vegetable. Cauliflower turned out to be a great candidate— it sweetens as it cooks and caramelizes, and the myriad seasonings cling to the florets and their itty bitty crevices. Thus my mash-up recipe was born.

PREP TIME: 10 MINUTES

COOK TIME: 15 MINUTES

MAKES: 4 SERVINGS

3 tablespoons vegetable oil,
   divided
1 large cauliflower (1¾ lbs/
   875 g), cut into florets
¼ teaspoon fine sea salt
1 tablespoon unsalted butter
6 cloves garlic, smashed and
   peeled
1 tablespoon grated fresh
   ginger
1½ cups (180 g) thinly sliced
   shallots
2 fresh long red chilies like
   Fresno, stemmed and seeded
   as desired, thinly sliced
¼ cup (60 ml) soy sauce
2 tablespoons granulated sugar
2 tablespoons whole black
   peppercorns, crushed
¼ teaspoon coriander seeds,
   crushed
4 green onions (scallions), cut
   into 2-in (5-cm) segments
¼ cup (5 g) coriander leaves
   (cilantro)

Swirl 2 tablespoons of the oil into a large wok or skillet and set over high heat until shimmering hot. Add the cauliflower, sprinkle with salt and stir to mix. Cover and let the florets cook without stirring for 2 minutes, until they char lightly on the underside. Toss and let the other side char, another 1 to 2 minutes. Scoop out the cauliflower and set aside.

Wipe out the wok and melt the butter with the remaining 1 tablespoon oil over medium heat. Add the garlic, ginger, shallots and chilies. Fry until the shallots have softened, 5 to 6 minutes. Stir in the soy sauce and sugar, followed by the crushed black pepper and coriander seeds. Continue to cook, stirring, until aromatic.

Return the cooked cauliflower to the wok. Toss to coat with the seasonings and cook until heated through, 1 to 2 minutes. Add the green onions and stir once or twice more. Remove from heat and transfer to a serving dish. Garnish with coriander leaves and serve hot with steamed jasmine rice.

Burmese-Style Pumpkin and Parsnip Curry

In Asia, winter squashes are generically called pumpkins—hence the name of this dish. If you've never had them, Burmese curries are very mellow compared to their Indian and Thai counterparts, and use less herbs and spices. Paprika is added more for color, so if you want to dial up the heat, substitute ground chili powder for up to half the paprika. Other vegetables that would taste great in this curry include cauliflower, sweet potatoes and carrots, but note that cooking times will vary.

PREP TIME: 20 MINUTES
COOK TIME: 30 MINUTES
MAKES: 4 TO 6 SERVINGS

1 medium (2½ lbs/1.25 kg) winter
   squash such as kabocha
½ lb (250 g) parsnips
2 tablespoons vegetable oil
1 cup (250 g) chopped yellow onion
1 tablespoon minced garlic
1 tablespoon minced fresh ginger
2 teaspoons ground turmeric powder
1 tablespoon ground sweet paprika
   powder
2 tablespoons soy sauce
3 cups (750 ml) water
Fine sea salt
¼ cup (5 g) cilantro leaves or parsley
   leaves, for garnish

Peel the squash and parsnip. Halve the squash and remove the seeds. Cut the vegetables into 2 x 1-in (5 x 2.5-cm) pieces.

Swirl the oil into a large heavy pot or Dutch oven and set over medium heat until shimmering hot. Fry the onion, garlic, and ginger until the onion is translucent and ruffled with brown edges, 3 to 4 minutes. Stir in the turmeric and mix well.

Add the parsnip, paprika and soy sauce to the pot and raise the heat to medium-high. Stir and cook until well combined. Add the water and bring to a boil, then reduce the heat to a simmer. Cover and simmer for 5 minutes, then add the squash and simmer for another 15 to 25 minutes. The curry is done when the parsnip and squash are tender and the gravy has reduced to about ½ cup (125 ml). Taste and add salt as needed. If there's still a lot of gravy left, remove the vegetables, raise the heat to high and cook until the gravy has reduced. Transfer to a serving bowl and garnish with cilantro leaves. Serve with steamed jasmine rice.

Tips You don't have to peel the squash if you don't want to, but be sure to scrub it thoroughly.
- Microwave the whole squash for 4 to 5 minutes to soften it and make it easier to cut.
- For a thicker gravy, add 1 to 2 chopped large tomatoes with the squash.
- For a protein boost, throw in one 15-oz (450-g) can of garbanzo beans (chickpeas), drained and rinsed, toward the end of cooking.

Note Outside the U.S., winter squash is called pumpkin. My favorite is kabocha, a squat Japanese hybrid with speckled green skin and sweet orange flesh. Kabocha is similar in texture and flavor to hubbard and buttercup squashes. Local pumpkins in Asia are a close substitute.

Winter Greens and Tofu in Spicy Coconut Sauce

This versatile dish can be made with any winter greens, from Swiss chard to kale to collard greens (my favorite). When available, green beans and chayote are delicious too. And if you are a pescatarian, add some shrimp to the mix. If you can't find baked or fried tofu, bake it yourself (page 43) or just use fresh tofu to save time. I prefer baked tofu to fried because it's less greasy, but either method gives tofu a firmer, meaty texture that keeps it from falling apart when simmered in the coconut milk.

PREPARATION TIME: 10 MINUTES (40 MINUTES IF BAKING YOUR OWN TOFU)
COOKING TIME: 20 MINUTES
MAKES: 4 SERVINGS

12 oz (350 g) Swiss chard, kale or other hearty green vegetable

2 tablespoons vegetable oil

1 clove garlic, minced

½ cup (60 g) thinly sliced shallots

1 to 2 tablespoons (or more, to taste) chili paste, like *sambal oelek*

2 teaspoons ground coriander powder

1 cup (250 ml) unsweetened coconut milk

1 cup (250 ml) water

1 plump stalk lemongrass, trimmed and smashed

½-in (1-cm) piece fresh galangal, peeled and sliced into 4 coins (optional)

8 oz (250 g) Baked Tofu (page 43) or Fried Golden Tofu (page 43) cut into 1-in (2.5-cm) cubes

½ teaspoon fine sea salt

½ teaspoon granulated sugar

Tear the chard leaves from the ribs and stack 3 or 4 leaves on top of each other. Roll into a cigar and slice into ½-inch (1-cm) ribbons. Repeat with all the leaves to get about 4 packed cups. Discard the ribs or save for another use.

Swirl 2 tablespoons oil into a large wok or Dutch oven and set over medium heat until shimmering hot. Fry the garlic, shallots, chili paste, and coriander powder for 3 to 4 minutes, until the paste is aromatic and turns a few shades darker.

Raise the heat to medium-high and add chard leaves a handful at a time, stirring constantly to allow each batch to wilt before adding the next. Continue to stir and cook for 2 to 5 minutes (cooking time varies depending on the type of greens selected), until the leaves are all bright green and wilted.

Pour in the coconut milk and water. Add the lemongrass and galangal, if using, followed by the tofu. Add the salt and sugar. Bring to a gentle boil, then reduce the heat to a gentle simmer. Cover and simmer for 15 to 20 minutes, until the greens are dark and tender and the tofu has absorbed the flavors of the sauce. Taste and adjust seasonings as needed.

Remove the herbs and serve over steamed jasmine rice.

Tip This dish is even tastier if simmered for longer (say, 45 minutes), or allowed to stand so that the flavors can develop.

Swiss Chard Brown Rice Sushi Hand Rolls

In recent years, I've seen several sushi innovations. Sushi made with brown rice, black cod masquerading as *unagi* (freshwater eel) and sushi wrapped in vegetables— think thinly sliced cucumber or vegetable leaves— instead of nori seaweed. This recipe acknowledges that some people prefer the more nutritious and fiber-rich brown rice to white rice, and that not everyone likes raw fish or seaweed!

PREP AND COOK TIME: 1 HOUR + 20 MINUTES DRYING TIME

MAKES: 4 SERVINGS (12 HAND ROLLS)

Sushi Rice

1 cup (200 g) short-grain brown rice or *haigamai* (partially milled brown rice)

3 tablespoons rice vinegar

1 teaspoon mirin (optional)

1 tablespoon granulated sugar

¼ teaspoon fine sea salt

Hand Rolls

6 large Swiss chard leaves (the leaves, not including the ribs, should be at least 9 in/23 cm long)

Suggested Fillings

24 skinny asparagus spears, trimmed

1 large red or orange bell pepper, cut into 24 strips

8 oz (250 g) store-bought or homemade Broiled Tofu or Baked Tofu (pages 42–43), cut into 24 batons (aim for 3-in long and ½ x ½-in thick, or 7.5 x 1.5 x 1.5 cm)

2 mini (4-in/10-cm) seedless cucumbers or ½ English cucumber, cut into 2-in (5-cm) matchsticks

4 oz (115 g) radish sprouts, tiny pea shoots, watercress or arugula (rocket)

Wasabi paste (optional)

Sriracha Mayonnaise (page 84), optional

Soy sauce or Homemade Ponzu Sauce (page 59), for dipping

Tips To get ahead, prepare the chard leaves, asparagus and tofu the day before; cover and refrigerate in separate containers.

• Most of the prep work (cutting veggies, making the seasoning, etc.) can be done while the rice is soaking and cooking.

• You can easily increase or decrease the number of servings depending on how many people you're feeding. You can also prepare all the ingredients and set them out for a sushi-rolling party!

• Other suggested fillings include steamed carrots, avocado, sautéed shiitake mushrooms, and ripe mango. Go crazy!

Begin preparing the rice (see sidebar). While the rice is soaking and drying, prepare the seasoning by stirring the rice vinegar, mirin, sugar, and salt together in a small saucepan. Warm over medium heat until the sugar and salt have completely dissolved.

While the rice is cooking, cut out the center rib from each chard leaf, leaving two long pieces of leaf. Bring a large pot of water to boil and prepare an ice bath. Blanch the leaves until just soft, about 30 seconds and plunge into the ice bath to cool. Spread the leaves on a clean kitchen towel and pat dry.

Next, blanch the asparagus until bright green, about 2 minutes. Transfer to the ice bath to cool. Drain well and pat dry. Set aside. Prepare other filling ingredients.

Once the rice is done, drizzle the seasoning over the cooked rice 1 tablespoon at a time, folding and mixing after each addition. As you mix, fan the rice with a hand fan or cardboard sheet to cool it down quickly and give it a glossy shine. Taste after each addition—you may not need all of the seasoning. Avoid adding too much or the rice will become soggy. Cover with plastic wrap until ready to use. (You can make sushi rice in the morning for use in the afternoon/evening.)

To assemble the hand rolls, lay 1 piece of chard on a clean, dry cutting board. Place 1 to 2 tablespoons of seasoned rice on the bottom third of the leaf and spread into a square. Dab with wasabi and/or Sriracha Mayonnaise if desired. Arrange 2 bell pepper strips; 2 asparagus spears, 2 tofu batons, 2 cucumber strips, and some sprouts on top of the rice. It's okay if some ingredients overhang, but don't overstuff the roll or it will be difficult to assemble and eat.

Fold the bottom of the leaf up and over the rice and roll and tuck the rest of the leaf around the ingredients so it's rolled closed on one side and open on the other, like an ice cream cone. Serve with soy sauce or Homemade Ponzu Sauce.

How to Prepare Brown Rice

Rinse the dry rice once and place in a medium bowl. Pour in enough water to cover by 1 in (2.5 cm) and soak uncovered for 1 hour. Drain the rice into a colander and set it over the sink to dry out for at least 20 minutes.

If using a rice cooker, cook the rice with 1½ cups (375 ml) water and set it to brown rice mode if there is one. When the rice is done, leave it to steam for an extra 30 minutes.

To cook on the stovetop, combine the rice and 1½ cups (375 ml) water in a medium saucepan and bring to a boil over high heat. Reduce the heat until the water is bubbling gently, cover with a tight-fitting lid and simmer until the rice is tender and the water is completely absorbed, 40 to 50 minutes. Take off the heat and let stand, covered, for 10 minutes. Yields about 3 cups of cooked rice.

When the rice is done, use a wet rice paddle or spatula to transfer it, still warm, to a bowl made of wood or other non-reactive material.

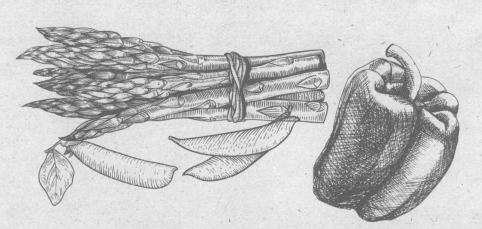

White Curry Soup with Pressed Rice Cakes

This delicious soup, called *sayur lodeh* in Indonesian, is popular in Singapore, Malaysia and Indonesia. My version is Indonesian-inspired, because that's what I grew up eating. Other versions may include turmeric or cumin—feel free to add these spices if you'd like. I love having chayote (known as mirliton in the American South) in this soup, but if you have difficulty finding it, substitute zucchini (and try to ignore that it's not in season).

PREP TIME: 20 MINUTES
COOK TIME: 15 MINUTES
MAKES: 4 TO 6 SERVINGS

2 fresh long red chilies like Fresno or cayenne, or 2 teaspoons chili paste like *sambal oelek*

3 cloves garlic, peeled

3 oz (85 g) shallots, peeled and roughly chopped

½ tablespoon peeled and roughly chopped fresh ginger

1 teaspoon ground coriander powder

2 tablespoons vegetable oil

2 cups (500 ml) unsweetened coconut milk

2 cups (500 ml) water

8 oz (250 g) chayote, peeled, seeded, and cut into 3-in (7.5-cm) matchsticks

1 small turnip, peeled and cut into 1-in (2.5-cm) cubes

2 medium carrots, peeled and cut into 3-in (7.5-cm) matchsticks

4 oz (100 g) green beans, trimmed and cut into 2-in/5-cm lengths

4 oz (100 g) firm tofu or tempeh, cut into 1-in (2.5-cm) cubes

1-in (2.5-cm) piece fresh galangal, cut into coins (optional)

1 plump stalk lemongrass, trimmed and smashed

6 oz (175 g) lacinato kale or other hearty green vegetable, shredded

1 teaspoon fine sea salt

½ teaspoon freshly ground black pepper

½ teaspoon granulated sugar

Pressed Rice Cakes (recipe follows)

Fried Shallots (page 26), for garnish

Tip Many other vegetables, such as eggplant (aubergine), cabbage, pumpkin or turnip greens, can be added to this soup. Be sure to add the sturdier, longer-cooking vegetables first and the more delicate vegetables later.

Make the spice paste by combining the chilies, garlic, shallots, ginger and ground coriander in a mini food processor. Blitz to form a rough paste the texture of oatmeal.

Swirl the oil into a medium Dutch oven or heavy-bottomed pot and set over medium heat. When shimmering hot, add the spice paste and fry until it becomes aromatic and turns a few shades darker, 2 to 4 minutes.

Stir in the coconut milk and water. Add the chayote, turnips, carrots, green beans and tofu, and bring to a boil, adding more water to cover the vegetables if necessary. Drop in the galangal, if using, and lemongrass. Reduce the heat to a gentle simmer and cover. Simmer until the chayote and turnips are almost cooked through, 10 to 12 minutes.

Stir in the kale, salt, pepper and sugar. Continue to simmer until the kale is just tender, 2 to 4 minutes. Taste and adjust seasoning as needed. If possible, let the soup sit for 1 to 2 hours so the flavors can meld.

To serve, distribute Pressed Rice Cakes among 4 to 6 large shallow bowls. Pour ½ to ¾ cup (125 to 200 ml) curry soup and vegetables into each bowl. Sprinkle with Fried Shallots and serve.

Pressed Rice Cakes

In Indonesia, these cakes, called *lontong*, are shaped into cylinders and wrapped in banana leaves. However, the technique is rather complicated and banana leaves can be hard to find. Here is a simpler method. If you can't— or don't want to— find banana leaves, use plastic wrap or foil instead. Note that the rice is meant to be soggier than usual so that the grains will compress and adhere together.

PREP TIME: 10 MINUTES + 2 HOURS SITTING TIME
COOK TIME: 20 MINUTES
MAKES: 4 TO 6 SERVINGS

1 cup (200 g) uncooked jasmine rice
2 cups (500 ml) water
Banana leaves, defrosted if frozen (optional)

Rinse the rice 2 to 3 times until the water runs clear. Cook in a rice cooker if you have one (measure rice using a standard measuring cup, not a rice-cooker cup), or on the stovetop, (page 24) with 2 cups of water.

To prepare the banana leaves, gently unfold them and run one leaf under hot running water to soften. Trim off the tough outer edge with scissors. Cut a length of banana leaf—it has to be big enough to line a loaf pan and have enough overhang, about 5 to 6 inches (12 to 15 cm), to fold over and cover the top.

Line a loaf pan with the banana leaf, shiny-side down (the side with the ridges). If it tears, just patch it with another.

While the rice is still hot, pack it into the pan, pressing down to compress. Fold the two ends of the leaf over so they overlap in the middle. Tuck in the edges. If the leaf isn't long enough, cover the gap with another leaf.

Leave to cool for at least 2 hours. (You can also refrigerate it to speed up the process.) If you leave it in the pan overnight, the rice will be imbued with the delicate, tea-like flavor and fragrance of the banana leaves.

Unmold carefully and peel off the banana leaves. Slice crosswise like a bread loaf and then cut into smaller rectangles or squares.

Tip If you are cooking for big eaters, the amounts in this recipe can easily be doubled.

Warming Vegetable Pho

To bump up the flavors in this vegetable pho recipe, I've combined the spices Andrea Nguyen, author of *Into the Vietnamese Kitchen*, uses in her chicken pho recipe—coriander seeds and coriander leaves (cilantro)—as well as those traditionally used in beef pho. You can use fewer spices if you prefer: 4 star anise pods, 1 cinnamon stick and 6 cloves; or use 1 tablespoon Five-Spice Powder (page 31) instead.

PREP TIME: 15 MINUTES + TIME TO MAKE TOPPINGS
COOK TIME: 1 HOUR
MAKES: 4 TO 6 SERVINGS

2 medium yellow onions, halved
Chubby 3-in (7.5-cm) knob fresh ginger
One 3-in (7.5-cm) cinnamon stick, preferably
   Vietnamese cassia-cinnamon
2 star anise pods
4 whole cloves
2 teaspoons coriander seeds
10 cups (2.5 liters) Mushroom Stock (page 29) or low-
   sodium Roasted Veggie Stock (page 28)
1 small bunch coriander (cilantro), stems and leaves
   (about 15 stems)
1 tablespoon fine sea salt
1½ tablespoons brown sugar
1 lb (500 g) dried flat rice noodles (*bánh pho*, page 17)
Freshly ground black pepper, to taste

Suggested Toppings

Broiled or Baked Tofu (page 43)
Broiled Shiitake Mushrooms (page 64)
Bok choy, Chinese cabbage, or broccoli, blanched (see page 41)

Suggested Garnishes

¾ cup (85 g) thinly sliced sweet onion, soaked in water to remove its bite
2 green onions (scallions), thinly sliced
3 to 4 chili peppers (Thai, Serrano, or jalapeño), sliced
2 large limes, cut into wedges
1 cup (100 g) bean sprouts
1 cup (20 g) mixed herbs: coriander leaves (cilantro), Thai basil, mint
Hoisin sauce
Sriracha or other chili sauce

Char the onion and ginger over an open flame on a gas stove (holding with tongs). Alternately, arrange the oven rack 4 inches (10 cm) under the broiler and preheat broiler on high. Place the onion and ginger on a baking sheet and broil for 15 to 20 minutes, turning occasionally, until sweet-smelling and charred on the outside and soft on the inside. You don't have to blacken all surfaces. Let the onion and ginger cool. When cool enough to handle, rinse with water and rub off any charred bits. Peel off the onion skin; scrape the charred skin off the ginger with a teaspoon and cut into thin slices along the grain.

In a 4-quart (4-liter) stockpot, dry roast the cinnamon, star anise, cloves, and coriander seeds over medium-low heat until aromatic, about 1 minute. Stir constantly to prevent burning. Add the stock, charred onion and ginger, and coriander stems and leaves.

Bring the broth to a boil over high heat. Lower heat to a gentle simmer, cover and cook for 45 minutes.

Add the salt and brown sugar. Taste. The broth should be quite salty to offset the bland noodles. Adjust seasonings as needed. Strain the solids and keep the broth simmering until ready to serve. You will have about 8½ to 9 cups (1.75 to 2 liters).

While the broth is simmering, cook the noodles according to package directions. Drain them well—you don't want to dilute the broth!

To assemble the pho, divide the noodles among 4 to 6 bowls. Arrange the toppings on top of the noodles and ladle 1½ to 2 cups (325 to 500 ml) broth into each bowl. Sprinkle with black pepper and serve with garnishes, hoisin sauce and sriracha in small dishes alongside.

Tip You can find fresh rice noodles (*banh pho*) in the refrigerated section of some Trader Joe's stores.

Easy Miso Ramen

There are two main components to ramen: noodles and broth. Proper ramen noodles, called *chuka-men* or *chuka-soba*, are the Japanese equivalent of Chinese noodles. Made from wheat flour, they are firm and chewy and stand up to the hot broth. Purists insist that mixed red and white (*awase*) miso should be used in miso ramen, and that it should be a little spicy. But it's up to you!

PREP TIME: 5 MINUTES + TIME TO
   PREPARE THE TOPPINGS
COOK TIME: 15 MINUTES
MAKES: 4 SERVINGS

2 tablespoons vegetable oil
1 tablespoon minced garlic
1½ teaspoons grated fresh ginger
¼ cup (50 g) chopped shallots
10 cups (2.5 liters) low-sodium
   Roasted Veggie Stock (page 28)
⅓ cup (90 g) white and/or red miso
1 teaspoon Homemade Korean Hot
   Pepper Paste (page 34) or chili
   paste like *sambal oelek* (optional)
2 tablespoons granulated sugar
2 tablespoons mirin
2 tablespoons soy sauce
2 teaspoons fine sea salt
½ teaspoon ground white or
   black pepper
8 to 10 oz (250 to 300 g) *chuka-men* or Chinese wheat noodles

Suggested Toppings
Charred Bean Sprouts (recipe
   follows)
Buttered Corn (recipe follows)
Quick Ramen Eggs (page 27)
Nori seaweed strips
Homemade Spicy Kimchi (page 39)
Soy Sauce and Vinegar Pickled
   Radishes (page 38)

Garnishes
Chopped green onion (scallion)
Crushed chili flakes
Sesame oil

Heat the vegetable oil in a large pot over medium heat until shimmering hot. Fry the garlic, ginger, and shallots until aromatic, about 30 seconds. Pour in the Roasted Veggie Stock and bring to a boil. Adjust the heat until the broth is bubbling gently.

Stir together the miso, chili paste (if using), sugar and mirin in a small bowl. Ladle about ½ cup (125 ml) broth into the bowl and whisk, then pour the miso mixture into the pot, followed by the soy sauce, salt and pepper. Stir to mix, then taste and adjust seasonings as needed. Keep the broth simmering.

To cook the noodles, bring a large pot of unsalted water to a boil. Meanwhile, pour some hot water into 4 to 6 large bowls to warm them. Cook the noodles according to package instructions. (Note: I like to cook my noodles about 30 seconds less than the suggested time.) Scoop them up with a spider or slotted spoon and shake to drain excess water over the pot (you don't want to dilute your broth) and distribute them evenly among the warm bowls.

To serve, pour 1 to 1½ cups (250 ml to 375 ml) broth into each bowl and add your choice of toppings. Serve the ramen with green onions, chili flakes, and sesame oil in small dishes alongside.

Charred Bean Sprouts

COOK TIME: 5 MINUTES

1 tablespoon vegetable oil
2 cups (200 g) bean sprouts
Pinch of salt

Swirl the oil into a large wok or skillet and set over high heat until shimmering hot. Toss in the bean sprouts and spread them out to cover the entire surface of the pan. Cook undisturbed for 3 minutes, then toss and cook undisturbed for another 1 to 2 minutes, or until they are nicely charred. Season with salt and serve immediately.

Buttered Corn

COOK TIME: 2 MINUTES

1 cup (300 g) fresh or previously
   frozen corn kernels
1 tablespoon butter

Melt the butter in a medium skillet over medium heat. Add the corn and cook, stirring, for 1 to 2 minutes, until cooked but still crunchy.

Tips Adding baking soda to the cooking water gives regular pasta the texture of ramen noodles. Boil dried cappellini or angel-hair pasta in water with 2 teaspoons of baking soda added per quart of water.
 • Have all the toppings ready before you cook the noodles. Make the charred bean sprouts last, because they'll turn limp if they sit too long.

Wintry Kimchi Stew

I make my own kimchi at home, and I usually finish a batch within a couple of weeks—certainly not long enough for it to ferment to the point where I don't want to eat it straight up. But once in a while (like when I go away on vacation, or have a baby!), I'll find a months-old half-eaten jar languishing at the back of my fridge. When this happens, I'll make this kimchi stew. Even if my kimchi isn't over-fermented, I still make it when I'm longing for a comforting stew.

PREP TIME: 10 MINUTES

COOK TIME: 25 MINUTES

MAKES: 4 TO 6 SERVINGS

2 cups (500 g) Homemade Spicy Kimchi (page 39)

1 tablespoon vegetable oil

½ cup (75 g) sliced yellow onion

4 cups (1 liter) low-sodium vegetable stock or Dashi Seaweed Stock (page 29)

¼ cup (60 ml) kimchi brine

1 teaspoon fine sea salt

2 teaspoons granulated sugar

2 teaspoons Korean red pepper flakes

1 tablespoon Homemade Korean Hot Pepper Paste (page 34)

1 tablespoon soy sauce

2 teaspoons sesame oil

2 Swiss chard leaves or other winter greens, shredded

2 green onions (scallions) cut into 2-in (5-cm) diagonal pieces

8 oz (250 g) tofu, sliced into ½-in (1.5-cm) thick bite-sized pieces

Freshly ground black pepper, to taste

1 green onion (scallion), chopped

Toasted sesame seeds

Tips Although any type of tofu may be used for this stew, I recommend soft (not silken) or medium. These will absorb the rich flavors of the stew more readily.
- Try poaching some eggs in the stew toward the end of cooking.

Squeeze the Homemade Spicy Kimchi over a bowl to express the brine (reserve it). Chop coarsely. Heat the oil in a large heavy pot or Dutch oven over medium-high heat. When it shimmers, add the kimchi and onion and fry for 5 to 7 minutes until they start to brown. Pour in the vegetable stock and reserved kimchi brine and bring to a boil. Cover and cook until the kimchi is soft and translucent, 10 to 15 minutes.

Stir in the salt, sugar, red pepper flakes, Homemade Korean Hot Pepper Paste, soy sauce and sesame oil. Mix in the chard and green onions, and arrange the tofu in the pot. Reduce the heat to medium, cover, and cook for another 10 to 15 minutes so that the tofu absorbs the flavors. Taste and adjust seasonings as needed.

Transfer to a serving bowl and sprinkle with black pepper, chopped green onions and sesame seeds. Serve immediately with steamed rice.

Red Curry Noodles with Roasted Cauliflower and Rainbow Carrots

After I tasted cauliflower roasted till its caramelly goodness shone through, I became a convert. It's paired here with carrots in a robust noodle dish known as *khao soi* in Northern Thailand with cousins in Burma (*ohn-no-kauk-swe*) and Singapore (*laksa*). Pickled vegetables and crispy fried noodles liven up the party, creating a lovely mélange of contrasting flavors and textures.

PREP TIME: 15 MINUTES
COOK TIME: 45 MINUTES
MAKES: 4 TO 6 SERVINGS

1 small head cauliflower (1½ lbs/ 750 g), cut into florets
4 medium rainbow-colored carrots, peeled and cut into ½-in (1.5-cm) slices
2 tablespoons vegetable oil, divided
½ teaspoon fine sea salt, divided
Crushed chili flakes, to taste
12 oz (350 g) dried or 2 lbs (1 kg) fresh egg noodles (Chinese or Italian are fine)

Red Curry Gravy

2 tablespoons vegetable oil
1 tablespoon minced garlic
½ cup (60 g) chopped shallots
4 tablespoons store-bought red curry paste
½ teaspoon ground turmeric powder
2 cups (500 ml) unsweetened coconut milk, divided
2 cups (500 ml) low-sodium vegetable stock
3 tablespoons soy sauce
1 teaspoon granulated sugar

Garnishes

2 cups (120 g) store-bought fried noodles (or use ¼ recipe noodle nests on page 91)
1 cup (150 g) Chinese pickled vegetables like baby bok choy (page 41), rinsed and chopped
¼ cup (50 g) thinly sliced sweet onion, soaked in water to remove some bite
Chopped coriander leaves (cilantro)
Chopped green onion (scallion)
2 large limes, cut into wedges
Soy sauce
Crushed chili flakes

Tips
To save time, roast the vegetables and boil the noodles the night before. Heat the vegetables up in the microwave and revive the noodles by dunking briefly in a pot of boiling water.

• If you're gluten-free, substitute rice noodles for the egg noodles. If you use skinny rice vermicelli noodles, La Choy brand sells crunchy fried noodles labeled "Chow Mein Noodles" at many grocery stores.

Preheat oven to 400°F (205°C). Arrange the cauliflower and carrots in one layer on two separate foil-lined baking sheets. Drizzle each sheet with 1 tablespoon oil and season with ¼ teaspoon sea salt and chili flakes, to taste. Toss to coat evenly. Roast for 15 minutes, then turn the vegetables. Roast the carrots for another 10 minutes and the cauliflower for another 20 minutes, until tender and caramelized. When done, tent with foil to keep warm. (This step can be done up to a day ahead.)

While the vegetables are roasting, make the Red Curry Gravy. Heat the 2 tablespoons oil over medium-high heat in a heavy-bottomed pot until shimmering hot. Fry the garlic and shallots until aromatic, about 30 seconds. Stir in the red curry paste and turmeric and cook until the paste is aromatic and turns a darker shade, 2 to 3 minutes.

Slowly pour in 1 cup (250 ml) of the coconut milk, stirring to blend, and cook until the sauce bubbles. Let it bubble gently over medium-high heat, stirring often, until the red oil separates from the sauce and rises to the surface, about 3 minutes. Stir in the second cup of coconut milk and wait for the oil to separate again.

Pour in the vegetable stock and bring the sauce to a gentle boil over high heat. Reduce the heat to a simmer. Add the soy sauce and sugar and taste. The curry gravy should taste a bit too salty (it will balance out when ladled over the noodles) and a tad sweet, with some heat to it. Adjust seasonings as needed. Keep warm over low heat.

To cook the noodles, bring a large pot of water to a rolling boil over high heat. If using fresh noodles, rinse them first in cold water to wash out excess starch. Cook the noodles in the boiling water according to the package directions. Stir them as they cook to loosen and unravel them. Drain in a colander and rinse with cold running water.

To serve, divide the noodles and roasted vegetables among 4 to 6 bowls. Ladle ¾ to 1 cup (200 to 250 ml) of gravy into each bowl. Garnish with the fried noodles, pickled vegetables, onions, coriander leaves, and green onions as desired. Serve with lime wedges, and extra soy sauce and chili flakes in small dishes alongside.

Index

ACKNOWLEDGMENTS

This cookbook has been many years in the making and I have so many people to thank for helping it come to fruition.

First of all, I'm ever so grateful to my mother, Juliana, for feeding my siblings and I fabulous meals when we were growing up. It's because of her cooking that I have a penchant for great food. Plus, she taught me how to make my favorite childhood dishes and gifted me her recipes in the form of a handwritten cookbook. Then, there's my dad, Rudy. He encouraged me to start a vegetable garden and came to my rescue many times, whether it was in the form of digging dirt or trapping slugs. He definitely sowed the seed for my love of vegetables.

And of course, a huge thank you to my husband, Omar, and son, Isaac, for eating (almost) everything I cook.

My gratitude also goes to Dianne Jacob for helping me polish my book proposal, and to my fantastic agent Clare Pelino for having faith in me and my work, and for always being on my side.

Photographer Sarah Culver and stylist Kelsey Mattson were truly amazing to work with! Thank you for being patient, flexible, and willing to work with me on the minutiae of Asian food culture and customs.

This book would never have happened without Debra Samuels. Thanks Deb for the Introduction.

Of course, I couldn't have done it without my recipe testers, both friends and strangers. Special thanks goes out to Laura McCarthy who was unending in her enthusiasm and energy to help me perfect my recipes.

Thank you: Marcie Flinchum Atkins, Betty Ann Besa-Quirino, Mei Lin Clark, Suzana Maria Dharma, Wing Fong, Patricia Holm, Wendy Kiang-Spray, Laura Kumin, Shirley Lam, Gerald Lim, Manda Mangrai, Lori Luster, Dotti McLean, Nicole Lalani Oandasan, Lani Randle, Julie Riley, Linda Shiue, Michael Stewart, Niki Stojnic, Kava Vale, and thank you to the Tuttle Publishing team.

DISTRIBUTED BY

North America, Latin America & Europe
Tuttle Publishing
364 Innovation Drive
North Clarendon, VT
05759-9436 U.S.A.
Tel: (802) 773-8930
Fax: (802) 773-6993
info@tuttlepublishing.com
www.tuttlepublishing.com

Japan
Tuttle Publishing
Yaekari Building, 3rd Floor
5-4-12 Osaki, Shinagawa-ku
Tokyo 141 0032
Tel: (81) 3 5437-0171
Fax: (81) 3 5437-0755
sales@tuttle.co.jp
www.tuttle.co.jp

Asia Pacific
Berkeley Books Pte. Ltd.
61 Tai Seng Avenue,
#02-12
Singapore 534167
Tel: (65) 6280-1330
Fax: (65) 6280-6290
inquiries@periplus.com.sg
www.periplus.com

Published by Tuttle Publishing, an imprint of Periplus Editions (HK) Ltd.

www.tuttlepublishing.com

Copyright © 2017 Patricia Tanumihardja

All rights reserved. No part of this publication may be reproduced or utilized in any form or by any means, electronic or mechanical, including photocopying, recording, or by any information storage and retrieval system, without prior written permission from the publisher.

Library of Congress cataloging in process

ISBN: 978-0-8048-4723-0

21 20 19 18 17   5 4 3 2 1

Printed in China   1612 XL

TUTTLE PUBLISHING® is a registered trademark of Tuttle Publishing, a division of Periplus Editions (HK) Ltd.

PHOTO CREDITS
Courtesy of the author: 6 (left and right), 7 (left and right), 50, 66, 92 (top)
Sarah Culver: Book jacket and pages 1, 4-5, 6 (middle), 7 (middle), 9-12, 13 (middle and right, top and bottom), 14, 15 (right), 16 (right), 17 (top right and bottom left), 18 (top left), 23 (top), 30, 32-33, 37-38, 40, 42, 44-46, 49, 51-52, 55-60, 62, 64, 66, 68-71, 73, 75-76, 78, 80, 83, 85, 87, 89, 91, 92 (bottom left and right), 93-94, 97, 99-102, 104-107, 109, 111-112, 115-117, 119-120, 123, 125-129, 134-135, 137, 139, 140-141
123rf: Paul Jantz 21 (center left)
iStock: jfmdesign 21 (center right)
Shutterstock: Te Berrie 18 (top right); Olha Afanasieva 18 (bottom left); Singkham 18 (bottom right); SOMMAI 19 (bottom right); jiangdi 20 (center); zkruger 22 (bottom center)

ABOUT TUTTLE
"Books to Span the East and West"

Our core mission at Tuttle Publishing is to create books which bring people together one page at a time. Tuttle was founded in 1832 in the small New England town of Rutland, Vermont (USA). Our fundamental values remain as strong today as they were then—to publish best-in-class books informing the English-speaking world about the countries and peoples of Asia. The world has become a smaller place today and Asia's economic, cultural and political influence has expanded, yet the need for meaningful dialogue and information about this diverse region has never been greater. Since 1948, Tuttle has been a leader in publishing books on the cultures, arts, cuisines, languages and literatures of Asia. Our authors and photographers have won numerous awards and Tuttle has published thousands of books on subjects ranging from martial arts to paper crafts. We welcome you to explore the wealth of information available on Asia at **www.tuttlepublishing.com**.